Choosing to Be Jewish

The Orthodox Road to Conversion

Rabbi Marc D. Angel

KTAV Publishing House, Inc.

T 23999

Copyright © 2005
Marc D. Angel

Library of Congress Cataloging-in-Publication Data

Angel, Marc.
  Choosing to be Jewish : the Orthodox road to conversion / Marc D. Angel.
    p. cm.
  ISBN 0-88125-890-3
  1. Conversion—Judaism. 2. Jewish converts. 3. Orthodox Judaism—
Customs and practices. I. Title.
BM645.C6A54 2005
296.7'14—dc22

                                                        2005009400

Manufactured in the United States of America
KTAV Publishing House, 930 Newark Avenue, Jersey City, NJ 07306

Table of Contents

Acknowledgments

This book is the result of nearly thirty-five years of study and experience as an Orthodox rabbi. I thank the many teachers and colleagues who have contributed to my understanding of conversion according to halakha. I thank the candidates for conversion who turned to me for guidance, and who provided essential insight into the conversion process. I am especially grateful to the converts who submitted essays for this volume, because their writings will enable readers to gain direct information about conversion from the perspective of those who have actually converted according to halakha.

I thank my wife, Gilda, and our son, Rabbi Hayyim Angel, for having read the manuscript of this book and offered their comments and corrections. I gratefully acknowledge the enthusiasm and friendship of Bernard Scharfstein of Ktav Publishing House, and thank him and his staff for producing this volume.

I thank the Almighty for having granted me the opportunity to present this book to the public. It was written for the sake of Heaven and for the sake of the honor and spiritual strength of the Jewish people.

Rabbi Marc D. Angel
Erev Shabuoth 5764

Chapter One

Conversion to Judaism in Modern Times

Every year, thousands of people throughout the world convert to Judaism. They come from different religious backgrounds, races, geographical locations, sociological conditions. Most tend to be well-educated.

They are drawn to Judaism for various reasons. Some are seekers of truth. They have grown dissatisfied with the religion or philosophy in which they were raised or to which they have been exposed. They have undertaken to study Judaism and to share in the life of the Jewish community; and they have found their spiritual home in the Jewish tradition.

Some, though born non-Jewish, have an almost mystical feeling that they really have Jewish souls. They have had a deep longing to become part of the Jewish people, and conversion enables them to fulfill this inner yearning.

Others have discovered Jewish ancestry and have decided to reconnect with the religious traditions of their Jewish forebears. One of the amazing phenomena of our time is the re-emergence of Judaism among people of Spanish and Portuguese ancestry whose research and family traditions have led them to reclaim the Jewish religion of their ancestors. They are descended from ancestors who were forcibly converted to Catholicism in medieval Iberia and were subjected to the cruel oppression of the Inquisition. Many fled to the New World, seeking a freer religious climate so that they might at least maintain Jewish traditions secretly. When the Inquisition also came to the New World, these crypto-Jews were compelled to keep their Jewish identities well hidden. Remarkably, Jewishness survived for centuries under these trying conditions—and descendants of crypto-Jews are returning to Judaism.

Some converts are the children of Jewish fathers and non-Jewish mothers. They may already have a strong Jewish identity, but since the halakha (Jewish law) defines Jewishness through the mother's line, they are technically not Jewish. Conversion brings them completely into the Jewish fold.

A number of converts undergo conversion for a second or even a third time. They originally converted under non-Orthodox auspices. As they study and grow in their Jewish knowledge and religious observance, they have decided to undergo conversion according to halakha before an Orthodox rabbinic court.

A number of people of non-Jewish background, wanting to settle in Israel, opt to convert to Judaism in order to feel more fully part of the Jewish state.

Some converts to Judaism are influenced toward conversion because they have lived among Jews and have felt comfortable and happy in a Jewish milieu. Conversion is their way to become part of the Jewish community.

A large percentage of converts choose Judaism for the sake of marriage to a Jewish spouse. They have fallen in love with a Jewish person or are already married to a Jew. In many cases, the Jewish partner (or the partner's family) is uncomfortable with interfaith marriage, and the non-Jewish partner agrees to convert in order to eliminate the problem of intermarriage. They feel that conversion to Judaism will remove friction from their marriages, and will enable them to raise their children in one faith tradition.

Converts: A Remarkable Group

Whatever the original impetus, those who convert to Judaism are a remarkable group of people. After all, the Jews are a very tiny percentage of humanity. Why should a non-Jew, who is part of a much vaster group than the Jews, consciously opt to become a member of a small minority? Moreover, the Jewish people are subject to overt and subtle anti-Semitism almost everywhere. Over the centuries, Jews have been persecuted throughout the Christian and Muslim worlds, and even today the ugly manifestations of anti-Semitism are all too obvious. The State of Israel is constantly under attack—physically, economically, politically. Anti-Israel propaganda and media bias are rampant, and the line between anti-Israel and anti-Jewish is blurry, if it exists at all. So why would a Christian or a Muslim willingly take on the real risks of being Jewish, in a world where being Jewish can be so dangerous?

Anyone choosing to convert to Judaism, then, must be a very special person. The prospective convert must be willing to leave a majority status to become part of a minority group. Converts must be ready to face the difficulties that may arise in relationships with members of their biological families who do not favor conversion to Judaism. The decision to become Jewish requires religious commitment, intellectual clarity—and a good deal of courage.

The great medieval sage Maimonides (Rambam) wrote a letter to a proselyte by the name of Obadya. Rambam underscored the unique qualities of the sincere convert to Judaism. Sincere converts, he pointed out, leave the family and community of their upbringing and undertake to become part of an oppressed minority. Their decision to convert to Judaism is the result of keen insight, commitment to truth, devotion to the Torah, and rejection of religions that themselves are derived from—and have altered—the teachings of Torah (i.e., Christianity and Islam). The convert has chosen the path of holiness, coming under the wings of the Divine Presence; the convert clings to the teachings of Moses and accepts the Torah's commandments. The convert's heart strives to come near to God, to bask in the light of the Almighty, to rejoice with the righteous. Such a person, wrote Maimonides, is "intelligent, understanding and sharp-minded, upright, the student of Abraham our father who left his family and people to follow after God."[1]

So imagine this: a non-Jewish person, after much thought and soul-searching, decides to take the great step of conversion to Judaism. This person approaches a rabbi and declares the desire to convert. Historically—and very often even today within the community that adheres to halakha—the candidate for conversion is not embraced enthusiastically, but is actually discouraged from converting! Following the pattern outlined in the Talmud (Yebamot 47a–b), the rabbi is likely to ask the candidate: "Why do you want to convert? Don't you realize that Jews are persecuted and oppressed, subject to so many difficulties?" If the candidate expresses willingness to convert in spite of these problems, the rabbi then explains some of the commandments that will now need to be observed, and the punishments for breaking them. "As a non-Jew, you are not obligated to keep a kosher diet; if you convert you must do so or be guilty of serious religious transgressions. As a non-Jew, you do not need to observe the many laws of the Jewish Sabbath; but if you convert, you will be obligated to keep them— or be accountable to God for your violations." The rabbi may inform the candidate that one can be righteous and beloved by God without converting to Judaism. One can follow the seven Noahide laws and still be rewarded with a place in the world-to-come. Heaven is not reserved for Jews only, but is for the righteous of all nations.

This response is often perplexing to candidates for conversion. They have made the extremely difficult decision to enter the world

---

[1] *Iggrot ha-Rambam*, vol. 1, ed. Yitzhak Sheilat, Maaliyot Publishers, Jerusalem, 5747, pp. 240–241.

of Judaism—and the first meeting with a rabbi is often discouraging rather than encouraging. Judaism, for most of its history, has not been pro-active in attracting and encouraging conversions to its ranks, and this is still largely the case within the halakhically traditional communities.

The attitude of Judaism toward proselytization is radically different from that of Christianity and Islam. Each of the latter religions views itself as having the exclusive truth. Their adherents are rewarded by God, and those who do not share their faith do not merit God's salvation. They feel driven to convert nonbelievers to their faiths, with the ultimate goal of having all humanity accept their religious teachings. Historically, Christianity and Islam have engaged actively in missionary work—often enough even using physical compulsion to gain converts.

Judaism, though, does not believe that everyone in the world needs to be Jewish in order to enjoy God's love and salvation. Rather, Jews must adhere to their own special covenant with God as defined in the Torah; and non-Jews are obliged to observe the seven Noahide laws, which include belief in God and maintaining a moral and just society.[2] Thus, Judaism has a far more universalistic and inclusive view of humanity than either Christianity or Islam, both of which seek to have all humans within their own religious fold. Jews do not feel an obligation to proselytize, since non-Jews can be righteous and God-fearing people without becoming Jews.

Consequently, non-Jews who decide to convert to Judaism do so from their own inner motivation—not because Jews have persuaded them to accept the Jewish way of life. This makes converts to Judaism all the more remarkable.

---

[2] The seven Noahide laws are listed in Sanhedrin 56a as the duty to establish a legal system to maintain civil justice, the prohibition of blasphemy, the abandonment of idolatry, the prohibition of incest, adultery, and other sexual offenses, the prohibition of murder, the prohibition of theft, and the prohibition of eating flesh cut from a living animal.

Halakhic and Non-Halakhic Conversions

Halakha lists three basic components for a valid conversion: circumcision (for males), immersion in a kosher ritual bath (mikvah), and acceptance of the commandments and tenets of the Jewish religion. A rabbinical court (Beth Din) must determine the proper fulfillment of each of these components.

While the process of conversion seems fairly straightforward, it has been subjected to considerable interpretation and controversy. Circumcision and ritual immersion are clear enough in their meaning. But what exactly constitutes "acceptance of the commandments"? Is this requirement satisfied by an affirmation that one has been informed of the commandments? Or by a general consent to be bound by the commandments? Or by a commitment to observe each and every commandment to the last detail? At what stage in the study of Judaism may a convert claim to "accept the commandments"? Can acceptance take place fairly early in the process, once the candidate has a general sense of the obligations of the commandments? Or can it only take place at a later point, when the candidate has studied more thoroughly? Or must it wait until a comprehensive knowledge of all the mitzvoth has been attained, a process that may take years?

Another area of controversy surrounds the definition of what constitutes a proper Beth Din. According to classic halakha, a person may serve on a Beth Din only if he himself is religiously observant. It is expected that one who officiates at a conversion should be well versed in Jewish law, especially including the laws relating to conversion.

The Orthodox Jewish community, with very rare exceptions, will recognize conversions only if conducted under the auspices of an Orthodox Beth Din. The rationale for this is clear: only an Orthodox Beth Din insists that its members be qualified according to halakha as codified in the classic halakhic works of the Jewish people. All the members of an Orthodox Beth Din are themselves religiously observant, accept the Divine nature of Torah, and recognize the authority of halakha and the classic codes of halakha. Since an Orthodox Beth Din functions according to the dictates of halakha, it has the authority to perform halakhically valid conversions.

To be sure, even within Orthodoxy there are variations of halakhic interpretation; not every Orthodox Beth Din functions with identical halakhic guidelines. Nevertheless, the overarching truth is that all the members of any Orthodox Beth Din are themselves believers in the Divine nature of Torah and in the binding authority of halakha—and they live their own lives in consonance with these principles.

In contrast, the Reform movement long ago abandoned the belief in the Divine nature of Torah and repudiated the binding authority of halakha. It has deviated sharply in belief and practice from the norms of halakhic Judaism. The Reform movement makes no claim that its conversions are conducted according to halakha; it holds that it need not to adhere to halakha in the first place. Even if Reform rabbis were to insist (and some do) that their converts undergo circumcision and ritual immersion in a mikvah, the rabbis themselves are not authorized to conduct halakhic conversions. Their beliefs and observances are not in accord with halakha, so ipso facto they cannot produce converts who are recognized by halakha.

Years ago, I participated in a public discussion of conversion among rabbis of different movements. I presented a range of halakhic opinions on the topic, in the hope of opening a reasonable conversation between the Orthodox and non-Orthodox on this touchy issue. The Reform rabbinic participant, though, quickly put an end to hopes for some sort of rapprochement between the Orthodox and the Reform. He stated: "I don't believe God gave the Torah; how can I ask my converts to believe this? I don't accept the authority of halakha; how can I teach converts to accept it? I don't observe the Sabbath or dietary laws or ritual purity laws in line with the halakha; how can I expect my converts to accept these observances? I only ask of the converts that they adopt a Jewish identity."

By self-definition, then, Reform conversions are not conducted within the guidelines of halakha, and thus understandably lack halakhic approval. The issue of the halakhic status of Conservative conversions is more complicated. The Conservative movement does claim to adhere to halakha, albeit to a halakha subject to revision based on the opinions of its own rabbinic authorities. Since the actual rulings and practices of the Conservative movement— including the permission to drive to synagogue on Shabbat, the seating of men and women together in mixed pews during synagogue services, and the ordination of women—are in sharp contrast to halakha as understood by the Orthodox, conversions performed by Conservative rabbis are generally not recognized by the Orthodox. But since there is a broad spectrum within the Conservative movement, with some rabbis being very close to Orthodoxy in belief and observance, it is possible that some conversions under Conservative auspices might receive de facto acceptance from the Orthodox.

For many years, the State of Israel sanctioned only Orthodox conversions. The rabbinate in Israel is overwhelmingly made up of Orthodox rabbis, and the Chief Rabbinate has always been an Orthodox institution. Yet, with the increasing complaints of the non-Orthodox movements—especially those in the United States— the State of Israel has been under pressure to revise its definition of conversion to include conversions performed by non-Orthodox rabbis. The non-Orthodox movements in Israel have strongly advocated recognition of their rabbis to perform all religious functions, including conversions.

The debate over conversion engenders considerable emotion because it involves the very definition of Jewishness and the authority to receive non-Jews into the Jewish fold. For the Orthodox, non-Orthodox conversions are simply not valid. Those undergoing a non-Orthodox conversion remain non-Jewish according to halakha. To call them Jews and allow them to marry Jews is a travesty that undermines the integrity of the Jewish people. For the non-Orthodox, the halakha (as interpreted by the Orthodox) is not the criterion for making a valid convert. As long as their rabbis approve of a convert, then that person is Jewish—regardless of the objections of the Orthodox.

While many prospective converts to Judaism apply to non-Orthodox rabbis, many others prefer to undergo conversion according to halakha as propounded by Orthodoxy. They understand that only an Orthodox conversion meets the classic halakhic requirements, and that only halakhically valid conversions can hope for universal acceptance within the Jewish community.

The Orthodox argue strenuously that conversions must be performed according to the age-old rules of halakha. Candidates for conversion should not be misled into thinking that non-Orthodox conversions have halakhic validity. To maintain the integrity of the Jewish people, those who enter its ranks as converts should comply with the halakhic process. Otherwise, a new status of person comes into being—a non-halakhic convert who thinks him/herself Jewish but who is not Jewish according to Jewish law. It does not take much imagination to realize how problematic this situation is, especially when the number of non-halakhic converts continues to grow. The definition of Jewishness affects marriage relationships, the Jewish status of children, as well as a host of other issues.

Although non-halakhic converts are not Jewish according to Jewish law, they have, at least in some important ways, left their former status as Christians or Muslims (or whatever other religion they had been practicing). They have taken on a Jewish identity, and have cast their lot with the Jewish people. It would be wrong to ignore the Jewish commitment they have demonstrated, even though they chose to join the Jewish people through a non-halakhic conversion. Yes, they are not Jewish according to halakha; but neither are they Christian or Muslim. They are in a new category, somewhat akin to the status of a *ger toshav* (resident alien). It is the task of the halakhic community to encourage such individuals to convert halakhically, thereby totally entering the peoplehood of Israel.

Responsibility of the Orthodox

Given how strongly the Orthodox feel about the need for conversion to be performed according to halakha, one would imagine that they would be actively engaged in reaching out to potential converts to Judaism. After all, conversion to Judaism is a significant fact of modern life. It involves thousands of candidates worldwide each year, and is not a phenomenon that can be ignored or swept away.

Moreover, the non-Orthodox—and especially the Reform—do view conversion to Judaism in a positive light. They receive candidates for conversion pleasantly, and even sponsor formal classes for would-be converts. One would expect the Orthodox to be offering candidates for conversion a positive, viable halakhic option.

The Orthodox are forceful in condemning non-halakhic conversions, and are equally forceful in demanding that conversions conform to halakha. The battle cry in Israel and throughout the Orthodox world is *giyyur ke-halakha*, "conversion according to halakha."

When it actually comes to providing a meaningful halakhic option for would-be converts, though, Orthodoxy is not very forthcoming. Instead of rising to the challenge of the non-Orthodox movements, Orthodoxy as a whole seems content to retreat to its own inner world. At a time when authoritative Orthodox voices are sorely needed to reach out to potential converts, the Orthodox community generally prefers to maintain the historic posture of discouraging them.

Many Orthodox rabbis refuse to get involved in conversion, or do so only rarely. The tendency in contemporary Orthodoxy, harking back to the rulings of Ashkenazic sages in the latter part of the nineteenth century, is to demand total halakhic observance on the part of candidates for conversion as a sine qua non of conversion.[3] Thus, those Orthodox rabbis who do agree to work with potential converts often set standards that are unrealistic for most candidates. By maintaining such high standards, these rabbis essentially convey the message that unless you are ready to adopt a total Orthodox lifestyle, don't even think of coming to us to discuss conversion. The entrance bar is raised as high as possible in order to exclude all but the few who are willing and able to accept the halakhic lifestyle in toto. This halakhic position, which began to take root only in 1876, veered from the far more inclusive positions that prevailed going back to Talmudic times. (This issue will be discussed at greater length in Chapter 4.)

The narrowing of halakhic options within Orthodoxy is evident from the following examples. In the rabbinical seminary of Yeshiva University, the bastion of modern Orthodoxy in America, a Rosh Yeshiva (teacher of Talmud) recently lectured rabbinical students on the laws of conversion. This was part of a series of lectures on "practical rabbinics." The Rosh Yeshiva told his students not to perform a conversion unless they were willing to bet $100,000 of their own money that the convert would be totally observant of halakha. One of the students asked: "Since no one can guarantee absolutely the future observance of any convert, doesn't this mean that Orthodox rabbis should avoid performing conversions? If so, doesn't this imply that we tacitly agree that would-be converts should go to Reform or Conservative rabbis?" The Rosh Yeshiva hemmed and hawed. Not wanting to state openly that Orthodox rabbis should let would-be converts turn to non-Orthodox rabbis, he nevertheless taught the class based on the assumption that Orthodox rabbis should never, or only rarely, do conversions.

---

[3] Tzvi Zohar and Abraham Sagi, *Giyyur ve-Zehut Yehudit*, Shalom Hartman Institute and the Bialik Institute, Jerusalem, 1994, p. 194. They point out that Rabbi Yitzchak Shmelkes, in 1876, was the first posek to define "acceptance of mitzvoth" as a total commitment to observe all mitzvoth, and to hold that a convert who did not keep all the mitzvoth was in fact no convert at all.

In the spring of 1992, when I was president of the Rabbinical Council of America, we organized regional conferences among our members to discuss the responsibility of the Orthodox rabbinate toward intermarried couples. It is easy enough to complain about intermarriage and its threat to the continuity of American Jewry. However, do we—as Orthodox rabbis—have a constructive role to play vis-à-vis those who are contemplating intermarriage or who have already intermarried? Do we have a message that might attract some of these individuals, perhaps helping them along the road to a halakhic conversion of the non-Jewish partner?

Many of the rabbis at these conferences felt that Orthodoxy's position is simple: Don't intermarry; if you do, you are outside the pale of the Jewish community. We have no responsibility toward those who have violated the sanctity of Jewish family law. If inter-faith couples turn to Reform or Conservative rabbis, that is their business—not ours. If they undergo non-halakhic conversions, this is their responsibility—not ours.

Other rabbis recognized a responsibility to intermarried couples, if only to keep their children within the Jewish fold. These rabbis believed that Orthodoxy must present a positive agenda, based on thoughtfulness, self-respect, respect for others, and religious integrity. While we must always insist on the primacy of halakha, we can still demonstrate an openness to the struggles of others and try to be of assistance.

The very fact that the Rabbinical Council of America sponsored these conferences became a point of controversy within the Orthodox community. The "right-wing" Orthodox groups attacked the RCA as having softened its opposition to intermarriage. They felt that just raising the idea that Orthodox rabbis might work with intermarried couples (and those contemplating intermarriage) gave a signal that intermarriage wasn't so bad after all.

Several of the Talmud teachers at the rabbinical seminary of Yeshiva University met with me to express their disapproval of the conferences. They said that Orthodox rabbis had no business discussing outreach to intermarried couples. These people were sinners, well outside the boundaries of the Orthodox community. They were not our problem.

I asked these rabbis if they had ever sat in the same room with parents who had come to them tearfully to discuss the pending intermarriage of one of their children; if they had ever spoken face to face with interfaith couples, or if they had any personal experience of working with people who were engaged in a serious religious struggle and had decided to convert to Judaism. The answer was no. I then asked: "How can you, who have never faced interfaith couples or their parents, pass judgment on this issue? You simply do not have the experience to know what is at stake." They brushed my comments aside. This isn't the Torah way, they assured me. Orthodox rabbis have better things to do than spend time with individuals who have so blatantly opted out of halakhic norms.

The critics of our conferences have grown stronger, not weaker, with the passage of time. The Orthodox rabbinate has become more and more concerned about raising the standards for conversion; and less and less responsive to the genuine religious needs of those who contemplate conversion.

Shortly after our RCA conferences, I wrote an essay that ended with this paragraph:

> There will always be critics outside of Orthodoxy who say we don't do enough and that we are too demanding; and there will always be critics within Orthodoxy who say we are doing too much and that we are compromising standards. Our task is not to let the voices of these critics divert us from a proper course of action, which includes absolute faithfulness to halakhic standards and sympathetic understanding of the needs of human beings. Ultimately, we are not answerable to our critics; we are answerable to God.[4]

---

[4] The essay appeared in a number of American Jewish newspapers, including the *Boston Jewish Advocate* of March 20–26, 1992.

The Structure of This Book

As an Orthodox rabbi, I believe that would-be converts to Judaism should undertake halakhic conversions. To do otherwise is to enter a limbo status in the Jewish community. The problematic Jewish status of non-halakhic conversions also affects children and grandchildren. By entering the Jewish fold in a halakhically acceptable way, one avoids a host of real and potential difficulties.

Moreover, the halakhic process is challenging, spiritually alive, and meaningful. It leads to a satisfying Jewish way of life that is all-encompassing and intellectually rewarding. It demands more of the convert, but according to the effort so is the reward.

In addressing the issue of conversion, we must be faithful to halakha. This entails knowing the range of opinions among authoritative rabbinic decisors as to what is required by halakha for a conversion to be valid. It also requires judgment as to which opinions are best suited to the contemporary situation and to each particular case.

Conversion, though, is not a topic that can be analyzed properly in the abstract, by merely consulting books and interpreting texts. Conversion involves thinking, feeling human beings who are seeking to find their way into Judaism and the Jewish people. We must be sensitive to the spiritual needs of those who choose to convert. What issues do converts face—with their spiritual identities, with their biological families, with the Jewish community, with their Jewish and non-Jewish acquaintances? What are the major motivations that impel non-Jews to convert to Judaism? What specific issues need to be considered when it comes to the conversion of children?

In nearly thirty-five years of experience in the rabbinate, I have had many opportunities to work with individuals who wished to convert according to halakha. I have had the pleasure of meeting halakhic converts from a wide range of backgrounds. I have asked a number of them to write essays for inclusion in this book, so that readers may gain first-hand perspectives from those who have chosen the halakhic way to Judaism through an Orthodox Beth Din. These essays provide candid glimpses into the thoughts, feelings, and experiences of individuals who have worked hard and sacrificed much to be part of the people of Israel. They demonstrate positive experiences with the Orthodox halakhic process of conversion.

The goal of this book is to present a meaningful, viable halakhic approach to conversion. To accomplish this, we must look into the halakhic sources; but we also must look into the eyes and hearts and minds of those who are remarkable enough to want to join the Jewish people. Conversion involves real human beings who have been raised in different traditions, who have ties of family and friendship with a range of people. It involves husbands and wives, parents and children, brothers and sisters. It is a process in which a convert undergoes a transformation and becomes, in many ways, a new person.

To meet its responsibility to the Jewish people today and to our future generations, the Orthodox community must address the issue of conversion directly, compassionately, convincingly. It must present a clear and appealing alternative to non-halakhic conversions. It must be willing to help sincere candidates achieve halakhic conversions. It must break out of its self-imposed shell and act boldly for the sake of the Jewish people.

In the August 22, 1986, issue of the Hebrew weekly *Ha-Doar*, Rabbi Joseph B. Soloveitchik—the singular leader of Modern Orthodoxy—was quoted in an interview by Rabbi Pinchas Peli: "It appears that 70 percent of mixed couples have a Gentile partner who is willing to become Jewish, and we have to be ready to accept them. We must develop programs and methods, integrate them [lit., draw them near] under the wings of God's presence [i.e., convert them], and to make of them good Jews. It is hard to get used to the idea, but this is the reality. Basically, this idea [of welcoming converts] is not bad. There are Jewish men, whose wives—born non-Jewish but converted to Judaism—have brought them [their husbands] back to Judaism."

Rabbi Soloveitchik, according to Peli's account, specifically indicated that the Orthodox community had to change its approach toward conversion. It needed to be more encouraging and responsive. It needed to reach out to potential converts rather than maintain the historical reluctance to get involved with conversions. It was mistaken if it thought that intermarriage did not affect their own community but was only a phenomenon among the non-Orthodox.

The interview with Rabbi Soloveitchik—a towering halakhic authority—has had very little, if any, impact on the Orthodox rabbinate and community at large. Even if he spoke candidly to Rabbi Peli, he does not seem to have articulated these views in his own articles and published lectures; and the ideas expressed in the interview have not become part of the mainstream of Orthodoxy, even among his most loyal and devoted students.

It seems to me, however, that the words of Rabbi Soloveitchik, as reported in this interview, are of great significance. They reflect the thinking of a Torah giant and communal leader: the situation vis-à-vis conversions is radically different from what it was in past centuries; it requires a change in attitude, and a change in action.

Let us study the halakhot of conversion. Let us hear the voices of converts themselves. Let us evaluate how we can best serve our people and our God.

Chapter Two

Historical Considerations

The Bible does not describe a formal process for conversion. The Hebrew word *ger* (in post-Biblical times translated as "proselyte") literally means "stranger" and refers to a non-Israelite who lived among the Israelite community. When the Torah commands compassion and equal justice for the *ger*, it is referring to these "strangers." But rabbinic tradition interpreted the word *ger* as also referring to proselytes, and insisted that converts be treated with kindness and fairness. It was deemed a terrible sin to insult a convert or to speak disparagingly of his/her past religious behavior before having become Jewish.

Rabbinic tradition actually includes two categories of *ger*. A *ger toshav* is a resident alien—a non-Israelite who dwells among the Israelites. Such individuals are not bound by the strictures of the Torah, but are expected to observe the seven Noahide laws governing moral behavior. A *ger tsedek* is a righteous proselyte who formally becomes part of the Israelite people and is subject to all the laws of the Torah.

The Midrash cites the origin of the conversion of righteous proselytes in connection with Abraham and Sarah, the founders of what was to become the Jewish tradition.

Said Rabbi Hunya: Abraham converted the men, and Sarah the women. And what does the Torah teach when it refers to "the

souls they [i.e., Abraham and Sarah] made in Haran"? This teaches that Abraham our father would bring them into his house, feed
them and give them drink, and demonstrate love toward them and
bring them near and convert them and bring them under the
wings of the Divine Presence. From this we learn that one who
brings one person under the wings of the Divine Presence, it is as
though he created him and formed him and fashioned him.[5]

Abraham and his family required the circumcision of males as
a requirement for entry into the Abrahamic covenant. Jacob's sons
insisted that the men of Shechem be circumcised, stating, "We cannot do such a thing to give our sister to a man who is uncircum-
cised" (Bereishith 34:14).

When the Israelites were redeemed from their slavery in Egypt,
the Torah informs us, a "mixed multitude" accompanied them.
Apparently this group eventually became integrated into the fabric
of Israelite life. Yet we are not given details about this, nor do we
learn of any specific process that the "mixed multitude" had to
undergo in order to become part of the Israelite people.[6]

The most famous biblical account of a convert is that of Ruth,
who followed her mother-in-law, Naomi, to the land of Israel. In
expressing her commitment, Ruth stated: "For whither you go I will
go; and where you lodge I will lodge. Your people will be my people, and your God my God" (Ruth 1:16). Ruth's acceptance reflected a commitment both to the people of Israel and to the religion of
Israel, the essential ingredients of a proper conversion.

The Book of Esther refers to non-Jews who were *mityahadim*—
"Judaizing." This may mean that they actually converted to

---

[5] Midrash Rabba, Shir ha-Shirim 1:3.

[6] Other biblical references to non-Israelites becoming part of the Israelite people
are Devarim 21:10–14 and 2 Melakhim 17:32–33. See also 2 Melakhim 5:15,
where Naaman accepts the God of Israel, although the Talmud assumes that he
became a *ger toshav* rather than a *ger tsedek* (Gittin 57b). The questionable status of Samaritans is discussed in Kiddushin 74b.

Judaism, or merely that they sided with the Jews, or feigned Jewishness out of fear.

When Ezra returned to the land of Israel after the restoration of the Second Temple in Jerusalem, he found that many of the Jewish men had married non-Jewish wives. He ordered them to "separate yourselves from the peoples of the land and from the foreign women" (Ezra 10:11). He did not advocate that the non-Jewish women convert to Judaism, but rather that the illicit marriages be dissolved altogether. It is not known, though, whether Ezra was ideologically opposed to conversion for the sake of marriage, or was simply taking an extreme measure that was needed in this particular situation.

Rabbinic Attitudes

While the Biblical record does not give specific guidelines governing conversion, there is no doubt that non-Israelites did become part of the Israelite people. In Talmudic times, when conversion procedures were delineated, it was generally assumed that these procedures also had been in effect during the Biblical period. Thus, it was taken for granted that Asenath converted before marrying Joseph and that Tsipporah converted before marrying Moses. It was likewise assumed that the foreign wives of King Solomon had been converted prior to their marriages to him. According to rabbinic tradition, all such conversions were performed according to the rules spelled out in the halakha.

Within the corpus of rabbinic literature, we find conflicting statements regarding conversion and converts. On the one hand, righteous proselytes are singled out for praise. The Amidah prayer, recited three times each day, includes a special reference to converts (*gerei ha-tseddek*). Indeed, the prayer lists them together with the righteous (*tsaddikim*) as worthy of God's compassion.[7]

---

[7] Megillah 17b.

King David, from whose line the Messiah will ultimately emerge, is a descendant of Ruth the Moabite, who was a righteous proselyte. Moreover, several great sages of Judaism were either converts or descendants of converts, among them Onkelos, who translated the Torah into Aramaic; Shemaya and Abtalyon, who were vital links in the rabbinic tradition and leaders of the generation before Hillel and Shammai; and Rabbi Akiba and Rabbi Meir, preeminent rabbinic sages of the Tannaitic period, who were said to have been descended from non-Jews who had been enemies of the Jewish people. Rabbinic tradition mentions a number of Roman nobles who converted to Judaism.[8] With such distinguished individuals in the ranks of the families of converts, it is obvious that conversion produced very positive results for the Jewish people.

The Talmud cites the opinion of Rabbi Eliezer that the reason the Jews were exiled from their land was so that they could gather converts in the lands of their dispersion.[9] Thus, the receiving of converts into the Jewish fold was a positive goal. Rabbi Hanina stated that many non-Jews converted to Judaism at the time that the Almighty did a miracle for Hananya, Mishael, and Azarya.[10] They realized that God was all-powerful and destroyed their idols. This was a positive development, in that non-Jews were inspired to reject idolatry and to become Jewish.

Rabbi Hanina also avers that a certain population of non-Jews was sinful and deserving of divine punishment, but the people were spared because they produced one righteous proselyte to Judaism each year.[11] This merit was so great that it averted God's wrath from them.

---

[8] Gittin 56a; Devarim Rabba 2:24; Shemoth Rabba 30:12. See also Louis H. Feldman, *Jew and Gentile in the Ancient World*, Princeton University Press, Princeton, N.J., 1993, p. 311.

[9] Pesahim 87b.

[10] Shir ha-Shirim Rabba 1:3.

[11] Ibid. 1:4.

On the other hand, rabbinic literature also reflects negative attitudes toward conversion and converts. Probably the most notorious example is the statement by Rabbi Helbo: "Converts are as difficult to Israel as a scab."[12] Rabbi Yitzhak warned that many problems will befall those who receive converts into Judaism.[13] One Talmudic statement went so far as to say that converts cause the delay of the arrival of the Messiah.[14]

The different views expressed in rabbinic literature reflect different attitudes among the sages—and among the people in general. Some were positively disposed to receive converts—and even to seek them out. Others were dubious about the value of accepting converts into the Jewish fold, let alone seeking them.

Although there were differences in attitude vis-à-vis conversion, the fact is that conversions to Judaism took place. Dr. Louis Feldman, in his study of the Jews in the ancient Greek and Roman societies, argues that Jews were actually quite successful in gaining converts. Given the estimates of the dramatic growth in the Jewish population during Hellenistic times, "only proselytism can account for this vast increase, though admittedly aggressive proselytism is only one possible explanation for the numerous conversions."[15] Josephus refers to the Jewish success in attracting proselytes.[16]

With the destruction of Jerusalem by the Romans in 70 C.E., the Temple in Jerusalem was razed. While the rabbis sought to maintain religious continuity by establishing a center in Yavneh, many Jews went into exile; life in the land of Israel was increasingly difficult under Roman occupation. This was hardly an ideal period to expect that non-Jews would be attracted to join the Jewish people—although some still did so.

---

[12] Kiddushin 70b.

[13] Yevamot 109b.

[14] Nidah 13b.

[15] Feldman, op. cit., p. 293. Chapter 9 of his book is entitled "The Success of Proselytism by Jews in the Hellenistic and Early Roman Periods."

[16] *Against Apion* 2:40; *The Jewish War* 2:20:2; *Antiquities of the Jews* 20:2:1–4.

As Christianity rose to power, its leadership sought to convert Jews to Christianity, and imposed sanctions against Jews engaged in converting Christians to Judaism. During the fourth and fifth centuries, these sanctions became increasingly severe, ultimately making it a capital offense for a Jew to convert a Christian to Judaism. With the rise of Islam, similar sanctions forbade Jewish proselytization among Muslims—also making such behavior a capital offense. Thus, for many centuries Jews throughout the Christian and Muslim worlds engaged in proselytizing non-Jews only at great personal risk. In those cases where conversions were performed— and there were non-Jews who converted to Judaism throughout these centuries—the Jewish authorities wanted to be absolutely sure that the converts would be truly faithful Jews. It was too risky taking in converts who might later revert to their original religions and cause great suffering for the Jews.

The Modern Period

In the eighteenth and nineteenth centuries, a spirit of enlightenment developed in Western Europe and the United States that gave expanding rights to Jews. With emancipation and citizenship, Jews gained the opportunity to participate actively in the societies in which they lived—to attend public schools and universities, hold public office, serve in the military, and so on. As Jews and non-Jews came into much greater contact than in former times, a new era began.

Among the Jews, an assimilationist tendency increased. Many Jews wanted to blend in with their non-Jewish compatriots. Some converted out of Judaism. Others chose to reform Jewish practices to be more in line with the patterns of Christian society. The Reform movement introduced changes in Jewish worship—using the vernacular more and Hebrew less, eliminating references to a Jewish homeland and messianic aspirations, having an organ for musical accompaniment in their temples, and even in some communities changing the day of Sabbath worship from Saturday to

Sunday. The Reform movement also gave up traditional Jewish religious practices such as the dietary laws, many of the Sabbath and festival laws, the laws of ritual purity in marriage. In short, the goal was to turn Jews into Germans or Frenchmen or Americans "of the Mosaic persuasion"; and to ensure that the Mosaic persuasion blended in as inconspicuously as possible with the prevailing social mores of the countries in which Jews lived.

Within the Jewish community, struggles arose between traditionalists and reformers. The rainbow of opinions ranged from the ultra-Orthodox rejectionists of emancipation to the ultra-Reform assimilationists. In this turbulent religious atmosphere, some Jews decided to abandon Judaism altogether—either by converting to another religion, or by simply being "neutral."

The growing interaction of Jews with non-Jews, though, also led some non-Jews to consider conversion to Judaism. Rabbinic responsa during the nineteenth and twentieth centuries reflected a dramatic increase in questions related to conversion, especially regarding interfaith couples. The modern era, which has witnessed the defection from Judaism of some born Jews, has also witnessed an increase in the number of non-Jews converting to Judaism.

The Orthodox rabbinate has generally maintained a cautious attitude toward conversion. Yes, they ultimately do welcome those who are willing to accept a completely Orthodox lifestyle. They are generally reluctant to get involved with potential converts who do not seem prepared to make the total commitment to halakha. In some communities, notably those under the aegis of the Syrian Jews, there is a ban on accepting converts altogether. They feel that by shutting the door to converts, they will keep their children marrying within their own community. None of the young people will even begin a relationship with a non-Jewish person, since they will know in advance that such a person would never be accepted in the community even after an Orthodox conversion.

An entirely different view was expressed by Rabbi Eliyahu Benamozegh, a towering intellectual figure of nineteenth-century

Livorno. He, too, was quite Orthodox in belief and observance. Yet he viewed favorably the growing interest in conversion to Judaism. This phenomenon reflected the ongoing relevance of Judaism to the non-Jewish society, and also Judaism's willingness to incorporate new people into its fold.

> It is not for nothing that over long centuries an uninterrupted flow of pagan blood has mixed with Jewish blood, and that each proselyte in becoming converted has contributed his own impulses and personal sentiments to the Israelite heritage. Jewish proselytism could come about only when minds on both sides opened themselves to giving and to receiving. Israel, having lost its political independence, has nevertheless imposed on its conquerors not its own laws but the Eternal Law. Nor has Israel failed to receive in exchange that which its own civilization was capable of welcoming.[17]

Since the mid-twentieth century, the phenomenon of non-Jews converting to Judaism has increased steadily and dramatically. This correlates to the increasing acceptance Jews enjoy in the United States and Western Europe, the rise of the State of Israel, and the greater number of classes and publications on Judaism that are available to the general public. It also is the result of the spiritual quest of sensitive individuals in search of religious meaning and willing to consider Judaism in a serious way.

A phenomenon of this magnitude and significance requires the studied consideration of those committed to the halakhic way of life. It is morally irresponsible to turn our backs on those who wish to join the Jewish people, and who desire to—or could be convinced to—join us by means of the halakhic process.

---

[17] Eliyahu Benamozegh, *Israel and Humanity*, translated by Maxwell Luria, Paulist Press, New York, 1995, p. 72.

Chapter Three

Conversion to Judaism from the Perspective of Converts

The preceding chapter dealt with Jewish attitudes toward conversion. For a fuller picture of the issue, though, it is essential to consider the attitudes of those who were not born Jewish but who decided to convert to Judaism. What attracted them to the Jewish way of life? How did they view the process of conversion? How did they incorporate themselves into the fiber of Jewish life? An awareness of the spiritual process of those who choose Judaism is essential if we are to understand the nature of conversion, and if we are to respond appropriately to would-be converts.

*   *   *

The following essay was written by a convert to Judaism who grew up in Holland and emigrated to the United States just before his conversion. The author is now married to a Jewish woman and is a student in an Orthodox rabbinical school. His spiritual journey provides a fascinating glimpse into the phenomenon of conversion to Judaism.

I was born and raised in a small village in the Calvinist Protestant part of the Netherlands, amidst almost every stereotype that is often used to describe the Dutch countryside: small houses, pastures with cows, dikes, windmills, wooden shoes, canals, cheese, and tulips.

My family was only moderately Calvinist. This consisted of praying before and after every meal, and (for periods of time) reading a piece from the Bible before saying grace. Our Sundays were mostly characterized by wearing uncomfortable clothes, going to church and Sunday school, and visiting family. Outside of our home, I was exposed to stronger forms of Calvinism. Most children I knew were not allowed to play outside on Sunday. Members of the stricter, conservative churches would not drive a car or ride a bicycle on Sunday. They were also recognizable by their dress code: the women were not allowed to cut their hair short (and would often wear their hair in a knot), they would cover their head when going to church, and never wear pants. Many of them, men and women, would only wear black clothes all week long. By wearing black, the strict Calvinists expressed their full awareness of deep and total sinfulness.

Calvinism believes that one needs to repent in order to be saved, but it is not in the power of man to do that. One cannot repent himself, but has to be repented by God. Calvinists traditionally believe in predestination. Thus, even before the world was created, God had decided who was going to be repented and saved, and who was going to go to hell.

From early on, I too was taught by neighbors, in kindergarten and later in school about the sinfulness of men, and about the punishments of hell, be it in a less harsh and upsetting way. I, however, do recall conversations with my grandmother, a very pious woman, when she said that a real place in heaven was too much for her to expect—if only she could stand at the doorpost!

Interestingly enough, because of constantly reading, telling, preaching and repeating the Biblical stories, especially the stories of the Torah and Prophets, Calvinists often feel a strong connection with Israel. In many Protestant churches in the Netherlands, there are regular fund-raisings for Israel.

As a young child I always felt very close to God. I loved the Bible stories about Abraham, Jacob, David, and Daniel. They were my heroes, and the God of Israel was my God. Even though I had been fascinated with the concept of hell and impressed with the sincerity and piety of some of the people I know, I never really believed I would be damned for eternity myself.

As a teenager, I somewhat lost my spiritual connection. My family had ceased to pray or go to church, and I felt that something was missing in my life.

When I was about fifteen years old, I came into contact with the Evangelical movement. Evangelicals are Protestants who accept the Bible as the word of God and the absolute, infallible source of Divine guidance. Their theology, though, differs from Calvinism in a number of ways. I was told by the Evangelicals that if I would give myself to God and sincerely accept His redemption, I would be forgiven all my sins and truly become His child. This message allowed me to recover my spiritual connection. I was overwhelmed with the feeling that God received me and loved me, that I was His and He was mine. Later, I was taught that this is what is meant when one is said to be "reborn." The Evangelical movement provided me with a way to activate and channel my spiritual energy, and made me feel part of a larger, worldwide special community.

At Evangelical meetings, there was a strong belief that God was truly present, just as real as He had been in Biblical times. People sang in exaltation, raising their hands, speaking in tongues, prophesying, having mystical experiences. These ecstatic experiences were felt to be a constant proof that it was all real and true. In the Evangelical movement there was a strong belief that God will do spectacular miracles for the faithful, including wondrous healings. Although I had ample reason to doubt the seeming miracles of healing, I knew no better way to maintain my relation with God than in this community.

Serving God was somewhat of a problem, because the message of the Evangelists was just too simple. All one needed to attain salvation was faith. Fine! But then what? If I want to dedicate my life to God, how do I serve Him? The problem here is that Christianity stresses faith, not mitzvoth (commandments).

(In Judaism, it is easier to find direction. If you want to be in God's service, there is no question what you can do. There are numerous mitzvoth waiting to be practiced: Shabbat, kashruth, holidays, family purity, Torah study, etc. But in Christianity, this structure was lost with the words of the apostle Paul, who claimed that "man is justified by faith, and not by the works of the Law.")

Evangelicals, lacking a structure of mitzvoth, stressed the obligation of preaching the Gospel and converting people to Christianity. Since this was the framework in which I then lived, I, too, preached the Gospel, going from door to door on Monday nights. I joined missionary groups, singing and preaching on the streets. I tried to influence Muslims, and members of my own family. I spent an entire year in a training school for Discipleship, entailing four months of full-time outreach to high school students. I taught children in Sunday school and I also was a teacher for adult Bible classes.

But in spite of this intense involvement, I was still not spiritually satisfied. I remember praying to God: "What is Your will for my life? How can I fully serve You?" I remember that at that time I also had a discussion about Judaism; my thoughts then were: For a Jew it must be so easy. They have the Torah and know exactly what to do!

As I grew older, my doubts about the Evangelical movement also grew. I did not see any major qualitative difference in the world due to bringing people into the Evangelical community. The only change I could see was that ordinary unsaved people now became ordinary hallelujah-singing saved people. I also wondered about the correctness of the teaching that only those who accepted Christianity would be saved by God, while all othes—who genuinely did not feel they could accept the Christian view—were doomed to hell. Moreover, the focus of Christianity was on being saved or not being saved—in the next world. But wasn't there also signifi-cance to this life, here and now?

I became more and more interested in the idea of living by the commandments found in the Torah. Since the Torah was the word of God, shouldn't it be natural for one who wants to serve God to obey the commandments of the Torah? The Christian argument that God decided to abrogate the laws of the Torah is peculiar and dan-gerous. How reliable was God, after all, if He cast aside the Torah whose words themselves testify to the eternity of the Torah? And if He could change then, what is to prevent Him from changing again and again? What is the possibility of attaining religious certainty if God Himself is so fickle?

Before going further with this essay, I want to describe another aspect of the village in which I was raised. In my neighborhood, there were a number of Moroccan immigrants. Having grown up in close contact with these Arab Muslims, I decided to study Arabic and Islam when I attended the University of Leiden. Islam and Islamic culture intrigued me. The beauty of the Islamic way of pray-ing was particularly attractive to me. As I pursued my study of Islam, my struggle with Christian theology intensified.

Islam taught that each individual prayed directly to God, with-out needing any mediator. This made sense. If God is all-powerful, surely He can forgive penitents without needing anybody to die for anyone else's sins. Islam's emphasis on pure monotheism made more sense than the Christian idea of a trinity. Interestingly, the Muslims are very close to Judaism in these points.

I was also attracted to the Muslim community, which has not suffered from structural secularization in the same way as the Christian world. Even the most confident missionary preacher could look like a doubting skeptic when confronted with an average Islamic man in the street. The Christian notion of building commu-nity on the basis of common belief is difficult to sustain. Since peo-ple believed and doubted in different ways, a community of faith is subject to disruption and dissolution. On the other hand, a community built not only on faith, but also on common religious practices, could hold people together more effectively.

Although I joined in Muslim prayer once, and participated in Sufi rituals several times, I never seriously considered joining Islam. First, the contents of the Koran are often at odds with the Bible, which I believed (and do believe) is the word of God. Muslims are obliged to believe in the Torah, Psalms, and Gospel as previously revealed Divine texts. But the many differences between the Koran and these texts seem to belie the Muslim claim. To counteract the claim of inaccuracies in the Koran, Muslims charge that their text is correct and that the Jews and Christians have doctored their own holy texts!

Moreover, the Muslims argue that God gave the Israelites the Torah, but then rejected them for their sins. He then gave the Gospels to the Christians, but then rejected them for their sins. Now He gave the Koran and Islamic religion. Using this model, though, one could argue that the fickle God—who has already changed His mind three times—may well change His mind again! So Islam may not be the final, permanent word of God—even according to the Muslim scheme of things.

Another reason that I felt unable to accept the Koran was the Koran's threatening nonbelievers with the punishment of hellfire, and granting Paradise only for the true believers. Threats and promises are not the purest motivators for proper religious life.

Since Christianity and Islam both accept the Divinity of the Jewish Scriptures, wasn't the Torah, in fact, the foundation stone of their religions? Any holy text that was possibly revealed after the Torah could thus never contradict it. In other words, if anything is true, it must be the Torah. Having reached this conclusion, I decided to go to the original source: the Torah.

At this point in my life, I had not met even one Jew. I stopped going to church. I started to reread the Dutch translation of the Torah, and looked for ways to practice the laws I read. I kept the Sabbath on Saturday instead of Sunday. I did not eat foods forbidden in the Torah. But I did not know very much of the implications of the written texts. I quickly realized that I did not need to study the Bible in a vacuum, and did not have to reinvent the wheel. There was a people who had many centuries of experience in fulfilling the words of the Torah: the Jewish people.

So now I started to read books on Judaism. I took Hebrew classes at the university (mainly biblical Hebrew and grammar), as well as courses on Jewish subjects. I began to attend Shabbat services in a synagogue in Rotterdam.

Soon after being in contact with the Jewish community in Holland, I discovered a few things. The Dutch Jewish community is very small and (especially the older generation) is still much traumatized by World War II. This may be one of the reasons why the rabbis in Holland are extremely reluctant to make converts. The practice is that a candidate for conversion must be approved by all of the main rabbis of the country—something that rarely happens.

At the same time, though, there are many people in Holland who would like to convert to Judaism. I personally know people who have been studying for more than ten years, living observant lives, keeping kosher, and so on, but who still have no prospect of conversion. I realized that if I wanted to become Jewish, it would be a really difficult road ahead of me.

If one wants to enter into the Jewish people, one has to accept Judaism as a whole. One cannot pick and choose what one will or will not accept. But having grown up in a scriptural tradition, I did not then understand the idea of the Oral Torah. I could not believe that there was an extra-scriptural Torah tradition with the same authority as the text itself. I was not then ready to accept this concept.

Although I didn't see any possibility of my becoming Jewish, I was determined to serve God and to follow the Torah. I thought I could follow the literal text as closely as possible, while still allowing for my own interpretation as to how the commandments could be fulfilled by a non-Jew.

This was a lonely position. Christians thought I was a Jew, and Jews viewed me as a Christian. The loneliness was not just spiritual but communal. How could anyone celebrate Shabbat or holidays without a community? I hoped and prayed that I would meet like-minded companions. Fortunately, I did meet them—people of different backgrounds, from different parts of the country, even from abroad. Each of us had thought that we were the only ones to have found our way to Torah without actually being Jewish. I remember the first time we came together—about seven or eight of us—in Amsterdam. We were happy and thrilled to have found others who shared our religious predicament. That meeting was the actual birth of a Noahide movement in Holland.

Our group originally called itself the "Alliance of Abraham." Just as Abraham had left his background, his old religion, and his culture to become a Hebrew (someone who crosses over to the other side to a land not yet known), likewise we had left our backgrounds behind for a yet unknown destination. Later, we changed the name to "Alliance of Noahides," meaning that our basis would be the Seven Laws of Noah, described in Jewish tradition as God's moral code given to the non-Jewish world. I published a monthly magazine named *Lekh Lekha* and organized an annual Noah feast around the time Noah left the ark. I organized conferences with various speakers, including rabbis.

It turned out, though, that the people who identified with our Noahide movement had differing goals and expectations. It is difficult to build an identity and found a community only on the basis of the Noahide laws. We revere God, we don't murder, we don't steal: yes, but would anyone think this code of conduct was so special that they would want to join our community? A religious community needs more than basic laws of morality. It needs a way to worship, to celebrate life-cycle events; it needs a religious texture for daily life.

Some of our group of Noahides wanted to develop their own system of mitzvoth as an alternative tradition to Judaism. Others hoped eventually to convert to Judaism. Others were perfectly happy just keeping the Seven Laws of Noah, and tasting bits and pieces of Jewish culture.

We tried to design an organizational structure that would allow us to develop our own identity. We imagined that Abraham himself had traveled with a diverse group of people who together came to form one camp. Every member of our group accepted monotheism as defined in Judaism, the Seven Laws of Noah, and a few other things. But we also had subgroups—called tents—each with its own specific ideals and practices. Each subgroup appointed a delegate to the Council of Tents; and we also had an Advisory Council, composed of Jews faithful to halakha.

I was part of the group that wanted to develop its own tradition, rituals, and prayers. In order to do this, I not only studied the Torah and Jewish tradition, but also alternative groups like the Karaites and the Samaritans. I read books about them and even visited their communities. I spent several Sabbaths with the Samaritans on Mount Gerizim, and also witnessed the bringing of the Passover sacrifices.

In consultation with others, I worked on developing ways to practice Torah for our small community. I composed a grace after meals, Sabbath prayers, and also developed various practices. For example, we would not light fire on Shabbat (later, we extended this to electric light), but we permitted transporting or extinguishing fire. We celebrated Passover with a stick in our hand and ate roasted lamb. We always celebrated Shabuoth on a Sunday, like the Karaites. I wrote a small daily prayer book, entirely based on the service in the Mishkan (the desert sanctuary of the ancient Israelites). We even had a place of worship in one of the rooms of my house that was a reflection of the Mishkan: curtains all around hanging on rings, supported by copper rods. We had a square tent-like structure in the front where we burned incense, and a menorah that was lit twice a day. For mezuzot, we had a card attached to our doorposts with the first two verses of the Shema, written in old Hebrew letters.

For all our efforts, though, things went wrong. If one bases himself only on the written Torah and is also a creative person, there are so many possible ways to interpret the text. Without a binding authority of some kind, all our rituals and interpretations were subject to constant change based on new insights or feelings. Because of so much fluctuation, the community could not hold on to a common lasting tradition. We had members who insisted on following a calendar not linked to the moon, observing the Sabbath only during the daytime, keeping Yom Kippur without fasting. Some began to object that the Jews had followed their rabbis rather than God. This line of thinking was intolerable to me. It led to my break with the group.

Over the years, I had continued to study traditional Judaism, and also did some lecturing on Judaism. I became chairman of an organization to rebuild an old dike-synagogue in my home region. Thus, my identification with Judaism had grown.

At last, I also began to understand the character and role of the Oral Law. I had seen clearly by my own experiences that without the Oral Law the tradition would simply disintegrate. I recognized that the rabbinical tradition is not really extra-scriptural, but is rooted in authority given to the rabbis by Scripture itself. The Torah grants authority to the seventy elders, and insists that their decisions be followed. The authority of the rabbis, the descendants of these first elders, is thus part of the written Torah itself. Furthermore, I realized that nobody can serve God and practice the Torah outside of the Jewish people. Ruth had first told Naomi, "your people are my people," and only then stated, "your God is my God." We can only fully serve the God of Israel by being part of the people of Israel.

Most Jews are born into Judaism. But strangely enough, some people have to go through complicated and long detours. It is said that someone who converts to Judaism was born with a Jewish soul that is restless until it finds its way back to Judaism. I believe that God has led me through unusual paths and guided me home.

To fulfill my dream of conversion, I needed to travel to New York. The rabbis in Holland created barriers that were all but impossible to transcend. I first was brought to an Orthodox rabbi whose goal seemed to be to prove that I was not a valid candidate for conversion. He asked me various questions, many of them quite technical, until he found things that I did not know in spite of my many years of study. (I never claimed to know all the Torah and Talmud; only that I had studied much and was prepared to keep learning and observing the mitzvoth.) The meeting was very frustrating to me, since I had genuinely hoped to receive a warmer welcome and greater encouragement.

Friends recommended that I meet with another Orthodox rabbi, and I did so. This rabbi was considerably more receptive, and very much appreciated the long spiritual struggle and study that had gone into my decision to convert. After having satisfied himself that I was indeed a sincere candidate for conversion, and that I had accepted upon myself to observe the "yoke of the commandments" of the Torah, he convened a Beth Din to oversee the technical aspects of the conversion. At last, I had become a member of the Jewish people.

The Shabbat after my conversion, I had the honor to be called to the Torah and read my own portion. It was the Parashah of Lekh Lekha, telling of Abraham's journey with God, the story that had originally inspired me to seek to serve God. As I read the Torah, I felt that Abraham our father had brought another believer—me—to his true destination.

*   *   *

The following essay was written by a young woman, raised in a Muslim family, who found her way to Judaism. It reflects various factors that affected the spiritual process—a thirst for religious meaning, a latent feeling of connection with Judaism, the influence of Jewish friends, and the decision to marry a Jewish man and establish a Jewish family.

Here I am, sitting next to my dear fiancé, J., in a taxi driving to
. . . where? Well, in a way, to the final destination of my journey
that started seven years ago, and to the actual beginning of the rest
of my life. Today I am going to the ceremony of my conversion to
Judaism. Some could call it a beginning of a new identity. It is not,
indeed. I think I always had it in me; things helped me realize that
this is who I really am. Yes, things, many things. A very close
Jewish friend from medical school (the only Jew in a class of 500),
the wedding ceremony that he took me to, an invitation to a Shabbat
dinner, then more Jewish friends, holidays, the history . . .

I did not just wake up one morning and decide to convert for
simply one reason or another. The more I learned, the more I found
myself in it. My interest in Judaism did not start with the intention
to convert. It was quite the contrary, indeed. Every little piece of
information that I learned has changed my life, added meaning to
my inner feelings; once I saw the whole picture in front of me after
so many years of looking at the pieces, conversion was just the right
thing to do.

I am from a predominantly Muslim country. It would be more
correct to say that I was Muslim by default rather than to say I was
raised Muslim. My parents are not fundamentalist Muslims, and are
not even close to conservative in their religious views. They truly
and genuinely believe in the one and only God. Beyond that, they
believe that people should be honest and good. They taught me
these values.

I remember a little incident from my childhood. I was six years
old, a year before I started elementary school run by the government. We had moved to a slightly fundamentalist neighborhood,
where all the children went to special programs to learn to read and
write in Arabic, outside of their formal school where they studied
in the Latin alphabet. To me, it rather seemed like a good activity,
so I wanted to go as well. My parents were furious when they heard
my interest in learning Arabic. They had a serious talk with me,

explaining that religion is important but that I would learn everything I needed to know when I started attending the secular, government school. We soon moved out of this neighborhood! My parents
did not want to have me influenced by fundamentalists. I was
raised, then, in a secular way, although we believed firmly in God,
the only God.

Having been raised with an open mind, I started to be interested in Judaism when I met my friend Y. in medical school. He was
the first Jewish person I had ever met, and was the only Jew in our
large class. Y. was a gregarious person, but was reticent when it
came to discussing religion. I pressed him with my questions about
Judaism, though, since this was the first opportunity I had of discussing Judaism with someone who was actually Jewish. He soon
recognized that I was genuinely interested in learning, so he started
telling me about the Jewish holidays and the related history. He also
explained his initial reluctance to answer my questions. Judaism is
not like other religions that proselytize, and is not actively involved
in seeking converts. To convert to Judaism is a long process, unlike
Islam or Christianity, where conversion can take place in a fairly
short amount of time. His comments served to make me even more
interested in Judaism. I tried to learn as much as I could about
Jewish life, and I could not help but notice the similarities between
Islam and Judaism.

It wasn't until six years after I had met Y. that he called me on
a Sunday morning to invite me to a wedding ceremony in the
biggest synagogue of the city. I was thrilled. I was so excited that I
hung up the phone even before asking what I should wear. I had
never been in a synagogue before, nor even seen pictures of a synagogue with people in it. I called him back to get those details. He
said: "Just be yourself. Don't worry, you will fit in naturally." I
will? I will fit in?

My legs were shaking as we walked to the synagogue from the
parking lot. I was holding Y.'s arm, with not a little anxiety. I

watched what everyone else was doing, and hoped I would not do anything wrong. I tried to pick up clues from the behavior of the others.

When we came to the entrance of the synagogue, the first thing we faced was a security check. Due to several anti-Jewish attacks in the past, the community needed to take safety precautions. Y. told me how security was a major issue for Jewish communities not only in our country, but throughout the world.

We entered a small room, accommodating six to eight people at a time. Two security personnel checked our ID cards, checked our names against the invitation list, and then kindly led us into the synagogue. As we entered the sanctuary, I sensed the fragrance of white roses and lilies even before my eyes saw the flowers. I'll never forget that moment. It was as though I were in a trance. Y. informed me that men and women sat separately in the synagogue, so I followed the other ladies upstairs. He told me that we would meet right after the wedding ceremony.

I found myself a seat toward the front so I could see the ceremony downstairs; but I made sure to sit several rows back so I could see the other ladies in front of me and follow their behavior patterns. I was immediately struck by how well dressed and modern everyone appeared, especially the women. I was impressed. Here was a religious community that was modern and civil. This is not what I saw among the Muslims among whom I had been raised.

During the ceremony, I obviously did not understand any of the Hebrew words. Yet deep inside I felt so peaceful. I could sense that my soul was relaxing. In the midst of the ceremony, I heard the name of the president of our country, and later learned from Y. that it was customary for Jews to pray for the welfare of the country. The Jews were especially grateful that our country had taken them in nearly five hundred years ago, during the time when Jews had been cruelly expelled by the Catholic monarchs of Spain. I was touched by this sense of appreciation.

After the ceremony, I met Y. downstairs and we followed the other guests to congratulate the bride and groom. As we walked through the synagogue toward the newlyweds, I felt a sense of holiness in the air. Y. told me that the couple had followed the civil law of the country by previously registering their marriage with the government. This, too, impressed me, since I knew that a significant number of Muslim couples did not bother to respect the laws governing civil weddings.

That day, Y. introduced me to his Jewish friends, including J. (who is now my fiancé). The young Jewish group were all highly educated, very sociable, and closely knit. I know a lot of non-Jews who have the same level of education and social skills, but there was something different about Y.'s friends. Their knowledge of world history and human nature made them all more mature, and taught them to be prepared for life—including adversity. They welcomed me warmly and invited me to their future gatherings. As we walked out of the synagogue later, I was smiling and thinking; not only did I fit in, but I also felt more comfortable among the Jewish group than in my own usual circle of friends.

Soon after, I found myself becoming part of Y.'s group—going to movies, dinners, recitals, art exhibits, and discussion groups. Then came an invitation from J. for me to attend a Shabbat dinner at his parents' home. I was thrilled and honored. He picked me up from my house, which was just a few blocks from his parents' home. As we walked, he explained briefly the meaning of Shabbat. He said that there are really two aspects: one is related to the religious message of the Sabbath, and one is related to Jewish family life. He expounded a bit on each of these elements.

J. explained to me that Shabbat begins on Friday evening before sunset, and lasts until Saturday night after sunset. Before Shabbat begins, it is customary for the woman of the house to light candles. Since J.'s mother had passed away a year ago, J. himself lit the candles and led the Shabbat prayers. He told me that he would say the blessing over the candles in Hebrew, and that he had prepared the blessing for me in transliteration so that I could follow along. I was glad to do this and wanted to know what else I should, or should not, do. He told me that I could respond Amen with the others, if I wished to do so.

His father, uncle, aunt, and cousins welcomed me with the warmest smiles. The ceremony went just as J. had described. I enjoyed being there and seeing how the family members treasured the occasion. J. reminded me that Shabbat brings strength to family life: it keeps family connected, aware of each other's lives, interested in each other.

One of the core elements in my own small family—my mother, father, and me—was our family life, our shared time together. We have always been strongly involved in each other's lives. So the Jewish Shabbat had a special meaning for me beyond its profound religious meaning.

My friendship with J. grew fast, and we became emotionally connected. But we never discussed plans for marriage, since we both know this would be a very complicated decision.

A year later, J. was accepted in an M.B.A. program in the United States. Ever since he had started college, he had dreamed of being able to study in America. Now this dream had come true. But the opportunity to study in the United States for an extended period of time also raised anxieties.

J. had always been an observant member of the Jewish community. He had planned his life based on the Jewish lifestyle, and had always intended to marry a Jewish woman so that he and his family could carry on the traditions of their long history. Now that he had met me, though, he had to grapple with the fact that he was in love with a non-Jewish woman. He made a radical decision and asked me if I would marry him. This was entirely unexpected by me, because I was already bracing myself for a break-up of our relationship. He then asked: "Are you willing to . . ." But then he paused. My heart was pounding and my inner voice was asking:

"willing to what? Please don't ask me to convert. I can't do it just for you or for anyone else. Religion is not about somebody else, it is you and your own faith, it is a deep emotional commitment. I could not convert for anyone else, only for myself." He continued: "You are in the middle of your residency program in the hospital; but once you finish it next year, would you be willing to move to the United States with me?"

I was still in a state of shock from the marriage proposal, and was struggling with a way to deal with our different religious backgrounds. I pulled myself together and said: "But how? I am not Jewish?" He smiled and said that he knew that by now. Then he went on: "We believe in the same God. You live your life according to the moral code of the Ten Commandments. I can't ask you to convert, because I could not do that for you either. Religion is something between you and God. I know that we will have a tough road ahead, but I am ready to confront it if you stand by me." I was relieved by his reply. I told him then—though I had not told him before—that I actually had been thinking about conversion to Judaism. However, although I had learned much, I did not know enough to make such a decision. I needed to learn more about Judaism, to determine whether it was really the right thing for me. I told him: "I will need your help along the way; but you should not put pressure on me."

A year later, we were both in the United States. He was in his second year of the M.B.A. program, and I had started working in the medical research center of a university hospital. The rabbi of the university campus was Reform, and a woman. Her husband was director of the Hillel office there. I introduced myself, and asked if it would be all right for me to attend services even though I was not Jewish. They were very welcoming, and asked if I was in the process of converting to Judaism. I replied that I had not yet decided, but wanted to learn and experience more about the Jewish way of life. I attended services regularly, and was especially moved by the services on Rosh Hashanah and Yom Kippur.

After attending Shabbat services so regularly, I began learning and memorizing the words and melodies, and began to participate with the congregation. I decided that I wanted to learn to read Hebrew, and registered for a Hebrew class given by Hillel. J. joined me for these classes, pretending that he needed to refresh his own memory of Hebrew reading. The class first concentrated on reading, but then we also learned daily conversational phrases. I knew I was making progress when J. and I were seated at a wedding near an Israeli couple and I could make some sense out of their Hebrew conversation.

My Hebrew teacher, A., became a close friend. She had grown up in Israel in an Orthodox Jewish family and had come to the United States to be with her American-born husband. Realizing my interest in Judaism, she frequently invited me to her home for Shabbat dinner and explained the various rituals. She even offered to bring me to Israel to spend time with her parents and friends, since such interaction would add much to my Jewish experience.

After Passover that year, I began to realize that the more I learned about Judaism the more meaning I found in it. I had been learning in bits and pieces. The time had come when I felt I needed a more structured training. I spoke with the campus rabbi, who told me she would be glad to supervise my training. We met weekly, and she gave me reading assignments. Our sessions ranged from theology to history to Jewish traditions. I took a class that described Jewish life-cycle practices as taught by Reform and Conservative rabbis. I came to understand that Judaism is a lifelong commitment, and that learning never stopped.

I wanted to be patient and to enjoy this training in Judaism without feeling rushed. I spent another year and a half taking classes and meeting with the rabbi. I continued to attend services and observe the holidays and life-cycle events. I was moving closer to the decision to convert.

One of my greatest achievements that year was changing my lifestyle so that I could observe the Shabbat. Most of the Jews in my university community were Reform, and a few were Conservative. None of them observed Shabbat in the Orthodox manner. I decided to follow a gradual process whereby I would increase my level of Shabbat observance. First, I gave up going out with friends on Friday nights; then I quit turning on television on Shabbat. Whenever I needed to work on Saturday—due to my workload as a research scientist—I only did my readings on Shabbat and avoided writing or using the computer. I did not cook on Shabbat.

As I increased my pattern of Shabbat observance, I found myself looking forward to it—it became my favorite day of the week. One Friday night, I stayed after services at Hillel to hear a guest speaker, a Holocaust survivor. He was a short, skinny old man. He talked about his years in Auschwitz, the years of torture he had suffered, the many deaths he had witnessed. His voice quivered as he recounted the horrors of those years. I had heard about the Holocaust and had seen movies about it; but hearing the story from an actual survivor brought tears to my eyes. I will never forget the pain in his voice.

That night, I decided to observe Shabbat in honor of this man. I did not even turn on the lights in the house. I spent Shabbat reading Torah.

Another year passed. I had made progress in building my Jewish identity. But since my training was mainly in the framework of Reform Judaism, J. was growing a bit concerned. He was from a traditional Jewish background and thought I should be learning within a more Orthodox context. He contacted his rabbi back home, and the rabbi referred us to an Orthodox rabbi who might be of assistance. We made an appointment with this rabbi, and the meeting went very well. He was calming and friendly. He asked how I had come to make the decision to convert. I told him that the process had actually been a gradual one, spread over a number of years. He explained the requirements for conversion, and asked me to read a number of books. He emphasized the importance of gaining fluency in reading the prayers in Hebrew.

He said: "I cannot estimate a time regarding how long this process will take, but we will see how things go." Then he added: "It is not usual to accept to supervise someone for conversion at the first meeting, but I see your strong Jewish identity, and I am confident that you will succeed. I wish you all the best." That was one of the most important moments in my conversion process. Somebody who did not know me before had now acknowledged the Jewish soul that I had nurtured in myself or—to put it more accurately—that I always had in me. And this acknowledgment came from an Orthodox rabbi!

I attended services in the rabbi's Orthodox congregation as frequently as my schedule allowed, because I was now living in another state. I observed Shabbat and studied Torah. I communicated my questions and concerns to the rabbi via e-mail. Everything I had learned before served as a good foundation for my new level of study and observance.

Within a year of my beginning to study under his supervision, the Orthodox rabbi asked me if I felt emotionally ready to undertake the conversion. He felt I had attained the necessary level of knowledge. He said that it would be nice if I converted before Passover (which was in two months) so that I could observe the festival as a Jewish person. I stopped breathing for a second. I was thrilled and honored and said: "Yes, I am absolutely ready."

We went over the details of the conversion ceremony and set a date for the mikvah. I spent the next weeks preparing for the ceremony, reading, thinking, being ready emotionally as well as physically.

Finally, the day came. Although a bit nervous about appearing before the Beth Din of three Orthodox rabbis, I reminded myself that I was well prepared and was eager to join the Jewish people. J. and several close friends accompanied me to the mikvah, for moral support.

I met the Beth Din; I reassured them of my commitment to fulfill the commandments of the Torah to the best of my ability, and stated that I was undertaking the conversion of my own free will. I then went with the mikvah lady to prepare for the ritual immersion.

As I entered the water of the mikvah, I felt a warm feeling wrapped around me, as though I were in the arms of God, the only God. I said the blessing and immersed a second time. When I emerged, I was Jewish!

Who am I? My name is Talia. I believe in God, the only God. I am honored to be a Jewish person and to share the faith and fate of the people of Israel.

*   *   *

The following essay was written by a woman whose initial reason for considering conversion was marriage to her Jewish fiancé. Her story is far more complex than the phrase "conversion for the sake of marriage" implies. My experience has taught me that many who start the conversion process "for the sake of marriage" undertake the actual conversion for its own sake.

I was born in Bacolod City, Negros Occidental, Philippines. I moved to Manila when I was nine years old. I have two sisters and two brothers. My sisters and I attended an all-girls Catholic school from primary grades through college. My father would not hear of his daughters attending a coed school even for college. My brothers attended an all-boys Catholic school. My family moved to the United States in 1980 due to the unsettled political climate in the Philippines.

Our family attended weekly Sunday mass and observed all the religious holidays. Daily prayers were part of our routine. My mother attended daily mass. With this background, I never imagined that I would someday convert to Judaism. Until the day I decided to convert, I regularly attended Sunday mass and continued to say my daily prayers. My prayers included a request that God find me a good husband. My prayers were answered when I met a good Jewish man.

The man who was to become my husband had not been raised in an Orthodox Jewish home, but it was tradition-oriented. His parents kept a kosher home, and his mother lit the Sabbath candles. He attended Hebrew studies after public school, Monday through Thursday, and on Sunday mornings, from age eight until thirteen. In addition, he had a private tutor help prepare him for his Bar Mitzvah. He did not attend weekly Sabbath services, only attending synagogue on the High Holy Days. He did not keep a kosher home on his own. When I met him, he was living alone and just over forty years old.

When we became engaged, we discussed the future of our careers. (I am a lawyer, and he is an entrepreneur.) We also discussed starting a family and what religion to raise our children in. I remember his words: "Not negotiable. They have to be raised Jewish." Although this was the first time he stated this demand, I was not altogether surprised, because I knew of his strong Jewish identity. He added, though, that I did not have to convert to Judaism. This was important to me, since I did not want conversion to be a condition of our marriage.

I began to think about how I could raise my children Jewish if I myself were not Jewish. I could not visualize my children attending Sabbath services in synagogue on Saturdays while I attended mass in church on Sundays. This was not my idea of how a family ought to function. I believe that a family needs a spiritual bond to keep it together. The way to achieve this would be to raise the children in a united home. With my conversion, I would provide the religious aspect of their Jewish heritage, and my husband would strengthen their Jewish identity.

I have close non-Jewish friends who are married to Jewish men; they do not raise their children in any religion. My friends have told me that their children are upset about this, and feel a void in their lives. I do not want my children to have that void.

There were times when I would wonder how I could give up the religion I had practiced since birth. Did my Catholic religion not mean anything to me? Was I willing to change my religion because of marriage? I discussed my dilemma with my family. I remember my mother saying, "We all believe in the same God, and believing in God is what is important." I was quite nervous about telling my older brother that I had decided to convert to Judaism; I was afraid he would stop speaking with me. He is the most religious in our family. I was very relieved, then, when he said that he was happy for me, and that I should do what would make my husband happy. With this support from my family, I decided to undertake conversion to Judaism.

My husband is not the first Jewish member of my family. My father's sister has been married to a Jew for over thirty years. My older sister had married a Jew, and recently they celebrated their twenty-second anniversary. Although she did not convert and her husband is not religiously observant, she herself does observe the Jewish holidays in her home. I discussed with her what Hebrew name I should choose for myself. I told her that my husband's Hebrew name was Moshe. She immediately said, "Then your name should be Tsipporah, like the wife of Moshe [Moses]." (We later named our sons Eliezer and Yitzchak Gershom, because Eliezer and Gershom were the names of the sons of the Biblical Moshe and Tsipporah.)

As a first step toward conversion, I read several books that explained Jewish laws, rituals, customs, and beliefs. I learned about Shabbat observance, the laws of kashruth, and the rules governing family purity and mikvah. Since my husband had been raised in a Conservative family, our initial thought was to have my conversion under Conservative auspices. We decided, though, to visit a number of Conservative and Orthodox congregations, sometimes on Friday night, sometimes on Shabbat morning. I wanted my conversion to be in a congregation where I would feel most welcome and at home. Since I am Filipina, I knew that I would stand out; but I wanted to belong to a synagogue where my background would not be an issue for me and my children. We wanted to have the conversion within a community that was accepting of us, where we could be married, and have our children's Berit Milah/baby-naming ceremonies, and Bar/Bat Mitzvah ceremonies.

After much deliberation, I decided to have an Orthodox conversion. An important consideration was that I wanted my children to be accepted as Jews in Israel, and among all Jews. My conversion began, then, for the benefit of children we did not yet have. My studies and experience led me to the conclusion that the halakhic route, the Orthodox way, was best for me.

My upbringing actually had things in common with the Orthodox lifestyle. I was raised within a traditional, modest framework where girls and boys were separated. I was not allowed to go on dates until age sixteen, and then only with a chaperone. Sunday was a family day for us, and my father never worked on Sunday. My mother would prepare special meals for our Sabbath, and serve them on her best china and on linen tablecloths. We would spend Sundays talking and reading, sometimes taking a family outing. I never worked on Sunday until I was living in the United States; I remember how guilty I felt the first time I worked on Sunday.

The Orthodox congregation we attended also played an important role in my decision. The congregants welcomed me. This was the only synagogue of all that I had visited where I felt at home. The warmth of the congregants helped strengthen my commitment. We became part of the community's extended family.

I studied a great deal, and began to learn to read Hebrew. Learning the prayers was the most difficult part; it took a long time for the Hebrew prayers to mean something to me. I found myself day-dreaming a lot while saying the prayers. Every now and then, I still miss the prayers I learned in my childhood. What helped me through this process was that the rabbi required my husband to study along with me. My husband's support and commitment were unflinching.

When I went to the mikvah for my conversion, I was accompanied by my mother, my sister, and my fiancé. When one understands the whole concept of the mikvah, it is a beautiful and meaningful mitzvah. This is a mitzvah I surely hope to transmit to my daughter. I had my three children in my late thirties and the last one just a few weeks before my forty-third birthday. I call all three of them my mikvah miracles.

As part of the conversion process, the apartment set up by my husband and me had to be kosher. Some of the kitchenware had to be discarded, some had to be made kosher, some had to be brought to the mikvah. We had separate sets of everything for meat and dairy. I learned to shop for kosher products, and how to identify which items were permissible and which were not. When the rabbi came to inspect our kitchen, he found it very much to his satisfaction.

While learning the rules of koshering chicken and meat, I told my teacher that I already knew how to do this because my mother had taught me to prepare chicken and meat in the same way. It turns out that my maternal grandmother's ancestors were from Spain. My grandmother had taught my mother this method of salting and washing meat. She passed away, though, when my mother was only fourteen years old. Had she been of Jewish stock, a descendant of medieval Sephardim? Other things came to mind that supported the Jewish-lineage theory. Circumcision was a must for each of my brothers. My mother did not cut our hair until we were a year old. On my twelfth birthday, my mother gave me a pair of earrings with a Star of David setting—I still wear them almost every day. She told me that on her wedding day my grandfather had given her a diamond bracelet with a Star of David setting, and the earrings came from this bracelet.

My teacher thought it was possible that my family was descended from Spanish Jews. I discussed this with my rabbi, who said, "Life is a circle, you return to where you started." I thought it was more than coincidental, then, that it was a Sephardic synagogue where I had felt most at home. When I discussed the possibility of

Jewish lineage with my immediate family, they accepted it as true, especially my mother.

My conversion strengthened my relationship with my in-laws. When we visited them in Florida, my mother-in-law was impressed that I knew exactly what to do in her kosher kitchen. She was proud of my being Jewish. When her friends said to her, "Your daughter-in-law is Asian," she would reply, "My daughter-in-law is Jewish." My in-laws treated me with much love, just as much as their other daughter-in-law, who is a very observant Jew.

The Holocaust was taught in my Catholic school in the Philippines from seventh grade. We devoted a semester in college to the Middle East conflict. I wrote a paper on the Jewish diaspora. Until I converted, I did not realize the enormity of the anti-Semitism in the world. Before I dated my husband, I was at a gathering and was speaking with a Pakistani doctor who had been born and raised in England. When I told him that I wanted to visit Israel, he said he would never speak to me again. I thought to myself that he was atypical. After my conversion, though, I began to realize how many people in the world feel as he did.

During the conversion process, I became more sensitive to issues of anti-Semitism. Because I am Filipina, a lot of people take it for granted that I am not Jewish; they feel they can express anti-Jewish feelings in my presence. Often, these comments reflect deep-seated anti-Jewish prejudices. I know that my children will face anti-Semitism. We have seen to it that they attend Jewish day schools so that they will have a strong Jewish identity to help them cope with this problem.

After we were married, my husband took me on a trip to Israel. We visited a second time and took our children, then aged four and two years old. A number of the tourist sites brought back memories of lessons I had learned as a child about the rise of Christianity. Now I was seeing these sites as a member of the Jewish people.

It is almost nine years since I converted. I have not regretted my decision for one moment. Nevertheless, there are moments when I feel sadness when it comes to the seasons of the Christian holidays that were such a central part of my pre-conversion life. I am no longer able to share these special times with my parents, although we do celebrate nonreligious events together. I know that my parents would very much want all their children and grandchildren to be together for the holidays; the magnitude of the commitment to convert hits me at these times. Also, I have no special customs and traditions from my childhood home that I can pass on to my own children. I have been fortunate in having parents and siblings who understand and accept my conversion, with all its implications.

My Orthodox conversion has led us to enroll our children in Orthodox day schools. At the time we applied to these schools, I learned that my children would not have been accepted had I not been converted under Orthodox auspices.

The Orthodox way of life requires enormous commitment, but the payoff is immeasurable—for my children, my husband and myself. Indeed, my conversion has brought my husband closer to his faith. My children are proud to be Jews, as I am.

*   *   *

The next essay is by a young man of Hispanic background, an attorney, whose road to Judaism led him to an Orthodox conversion, marriage to a Jewish woman, and the establishment of a Jewish family.

I was born in Los Angeles in 1967, the third of the four children in my family, and I grew up in East L.A. My parents had come to the United States from Mexico in their early teens. Though both are fluent in English, we mostly spoke Spanish at home when I was young. I grew up close to my mother's large extended family—grandparents, aunts and uncles, cousins—many of whom lived close by. We visited often. Although my father's parents were Baptists, very religious and active in their church, my father is not a religious man. My mother is a devout Catholic; as a result, our household followed Catholicism. My siblings and I were baptized, went to confession, attended church, and received communion weekly; and we were confirmed. I was probably the most religious, as only I chose to continue my religious education beyond confirmation.

The first major change in my life came when my middle school vice-principal encouraged me to apply to prep schools. I received a full scholarship to a prestigious East Coast academy. Although it was an incredibly hard decision for my parents, they decided to send me. So, at the age of fourteen, I was no longer immersed in my family's daily life, but in the culture of a New England prep school. Though I did not convert to Judaism for another ten years, this separation allowed me to begin thinking more independently about my faith and searching for my own answers.

I have always felt a strong need for spirituality and connecting with God, but as I reached adulthood I started to question—and then to doubt—many essential aspects of Christianity. Although I strove to learn more about the Catholic Church, my doubts gradually turned into disbelief. Later, I came to resent the church for its role in Spain's conquest of Mexico. By the time I entered college, I no longer attended church or practiced any of the sacraments.

In college, I studied anthropology and was exposed to various Eastern belief systems through friends; but I could not believe in them because I felt a strong belief in one God. Though I no longer practiced Catholicism, I still valued tradition and history.

Although I went to a college that had a large Jewish population, I didn't happen to form any close relationships with Jews and probably never met an Orthodox Jew. My first real knowledge of Judaism came after I graduated college. A friend of mine began conversion classes under Conservative Jewish auspices because her fiancé was Jewish. During her conversion lessons, though, she and her fiancé broke off their relationship. She wanted to complete the conversion process nonetheless. To help her through the process, I accompanied her to a few gatherings and meetings. One day, I went with her to Shabbat morning services at her synagogue. What I experienced there awakened something in me that I had not felt in years. Seeing families worshiping together, and listening to a beautiful sermon about tradition and community, made me think that perhaps this was something of which I could become part. After learning a bit more on my own and attending several more services, I decided to learn more about conversion.

I initially attended conversion classes at the University of Judaism in Los Angeles, a Conservative institution. I enjoyed the weekly classes taught by a kindly elderly rabbi. He brought the prayers and customs to life with stories of his youth, his own children and grandchildren. I recall a story he told about how his home once lost electrical power. He went to check the fuse box, and when he returned found his young children gathered around some candles he had lit for illumination: they were holding hands and singing Shabbat songs!

By far the most difficult aspect of the conversion was experiencing an adult circumcision. Though I feared the physical and mental trauma, I had learned in my classes that circumcision was an absolute requirement of halakhic conversion. I knew that if I were to convert, I would likely want to be a traditional, observant Jew. Once I was fully resolved that I would convert, I arranged for the circumcision. Although it was somewhat painful, I do not look back on the experience with remorse, since this was the gateway to the Jewish life, family, and community that I cherish.

Two years later, I moved to New York to attend law school. I attended services at several Conservative synagogues but never really found one where I felt I belonged. Perhaps I was self-conscious about being so different from most of the congregants at these synagogues. After all, how many Hispanic converts from East L.A. are there in the world? A friend told me about a Sephardic synagogue, and informed me of its history and diversity. Though I was somewhat intimidated by the fact that it was an Orthodox synagogue, I went there one fall morning; I immediately felt like I was at home. Although my Hebrew was not strong and I initially found it challenging to follow the services, I was so taken by the sheer beauty of the customs and music, not to mention the sanctuary itself, that I became determined to pursue an Orthodox conversion. Through my desire to become a full member of this community, I challenged myself to improve my Hebrew, understanding of services, and level of observance. I soon became knowledgeable of and comfortable with the various aspects of day-to-day observance, and found that I could even read unfamiliar Hebrew texts with relative ease.

Soon after I completed my conversion under the auspices of this Orthodox Sephardic synagogue, I met the young lady who is now my wife. Later she confided to me that if I had not converted according to Orthodox standards she likely never would have gone out with me in the first place. We now are blessed with three beautiful children, the eldest of whom has begun attending a Jewish nursery school.

The greatest change in my life that has resulted from my conversion is observing Shabbat. Shabbat observance gives shape to my week, ensuring that I spend at least one entire day with my family and community, focused on Jewish ritual and traditions.

My closest and dearest friends now are those with whom I attend synagogue and spend Shabbat each week. It amazes me that I likely would not know any of them had I not converted. I feel that the Orthodox community is especially accepting of converts because of the deep respect afforded those who have chosen Judaism, and because religious observance—rather than culture or lineage—forms the core of Orthodox Jewish identity.

One unexpected change is that I have become even closer to my biological family since my conversion. My siblings and father were immediately accepting of my choice, and I am grateful for their acceptance. My mother was initially hurt by my decision, but ultimately her concern was that I stay close to the family. Once she saw that I maintained my relationships with her, my father, my brother and sisters, and extended family, she has become incredibly supportive. She has been to my home and has seen how Judaism's focus on family and values affects the way I spend time with my wife and children. Her respect and efforts to accommodate my religious needs have been exceptional. When my wife and children and I visited her last Thanksgiving, she koshered her oven per my detailed instructions, bought all new pots and utensils, traveled across town to buy a kasher turkey, and prepared an entirely kasher Thanksgiving dinner for the whole family. Since Hanukkah overlapped with Thanksgiving, she carefully watched my wife prepare latkes and then she herself made them for us each day we were there. In this way, my conversion has given me the opportunity to experience acts of kindness, love, and devotion I would not have otherwise.

Chapter Four

Conversion According to Halakha

The primary sources for the laws of conversion are in the Talmud. The basic description of the conversion ritual is recorded in the following passage:

> Our rabbis taught: If at the present time a person desires to become a proselyte, he is to be addressed as follows: Why do you come to be a proselyte? Do you not know that Israel at the present time is persecuted and oppressed, despised, harassed, and overcome by afflictions? If he replies, I know and yet am unworthy [but still wish to convert], he is accepted forthwith, and is given instruction in some of the minor and some of the major commandments. . . . And as he is informed of the punishment for the transgression of the commandments, so is he informed of the reward granted for their fulfillment. . . . He is not, however, to be persuaded or dissuaded too much. If he accepted, he is circumcised forthwith. . . . As soon as he is healed, arrangements are made for his immediate ablution [in a mikvah]. When he comes up after his ablution, he is deemed to be an Israelite in all respects. In the case of a woman proselyte, women make her sit in the water up to her neck while two [three] learned men stand outside and give her instruction in some of the minor commandments and some of the major ones.[18]

---

[18] Yebamot 47a–b.

From this description, it is clear that the candidate for conversion is informed of the risks involved in becoming Jewish (i.e., anti-Jewish persecution and hatred) and is also informed of some of the commandments—not all of them. The point of this procedure is to ascertain whether the proselyte is joining the Jewish people with a clear and free mind, knowing the physical dangers that face Jews and knowing at least some basic requirements of Jewish law. The Talmud does not require that the proselyte accept to observe all the commandments—indeed, the proselyte is not even informed of all the commandments!

What about cases where proselytes choose to become Jewish for ulterior motives? The Talmud discusses this matter in the following passage:

> *Mishnah:* If a man is suspected of [intercourse] . . . with a heathen who subsequently became a proselyte, he must not marry her. If, however, he did marry her, they need not be separated. *Gemara:* This implies that she may become a proper proselyte. But against this a contradiction is raised. Both a man who became a proselyte for the sake of a woman and a woman who became a proselyte for the sake of a man . . . are not proper proselytes. These are the words of Rabbi Nehemiah, for Rabbi Nehemiah used to say: Neither lion-proselytes nor dream proselytes nor the proselytes of Mordecai and Esther are proper proselytes unless they become converted as at the present time. . . . Surely concerning this it was stated that Rabbi Isaac bar Samuel bar Martha said in the name of Rab: The halakha is in accordance with the opinion of him who maintained that they are all proper proselytes.[19]

Rabbi Nehemiah argued that conversions for the sake of marriage, or from fear, or from any other ulterior motive are not valid. He insisted that converts come to Judaism motivated by spiritual considerations alone. However, the Talmud rejects Rabbi

---

[19] Ibid. 24b

Nehemiah's viewpoint. The halakha is that a convert's ulterior motive is not a disqualifying factor. A person is Jewish once he has fulfilled the technical requirements of circumcision and ritual immersion.

The debate between Rabbi Nehemiah and Rab seems to hinge on how each side views the conversion process. Rabbi Nehemiah thought that conversion was primarily the acceptance of Judaism. Thus, if the religious commitment was tainted by ulterior motives, the conversion was not valid. But Rab—and the accepted halakha— saw the conversion process as the means of bringing a non-Jew into the peoplehood of Israel. Being bound by halakha is a consequence of being a member of the Jewish people. But even if a person entered the peoplehood of Israel for ulterior motives (i.e., not pure- ly religious), he or she was still to be considered a valid convert, a full member of the Jewish people.

What if a convert's knowledge of the commandments of Judaism was minimal or even nonexistent? The Talmud states the rule that a person who unknowingly transgresses many Sabbath laws is only obligated to bring one sin offering rather than one offering for each transgression. Rab and Shemuel, the leading sages of their time, explained that this rule refers to "a child who was cap- tured among non-Jews and a convert who was converted among the gentiles."[20] These individuals simply did not know the Shabbat laws, because they had been raised or converted among non-Jews; they cannot be held fully responsible for their transgressions. The notion of a convert who was converted among the gentiles is strik- ing. This means that a non-Jew could accept Judaism and somehow manage to fulfill the technical requirements of conversion but not even know the laws of Shabbat, one of the most basic Jewish obser- vances. Such a convert would clearly not have received a thorough training in Judaism, and apparently would not even have the oppor-

---

[20] Shabbat 68a.

tunity to learn very much about Jewish law, but the Talmud accepts that such a person is a valid convert.

Maimonides provides a classic statement of the halakha:

> A proselyte who . . . was circumcised and immersed in the presence of three laymen is a proselyte. Even if it is known that he converted for some ulterior motive, once he has been circumcised and immersed he has left the status of being a non-Jew and we suspect him until his righteousness is clarified. Even if he recanted and worshipped idols, he is [considered] a Jewish apostate; if he betroths a Jewish woman according to halakha, they are betrothed; and an article he lost must be returned to him as to any other Jew. Having immersed, he is a Jew.[21]

The halakha as recorded by Maimonides is that a person who undergoes the technical procedures of conversion (i.e., circumcision and immersion) in the presence of a Beth Din (even one made up of laymen) is a valid convert. Such a person is considered a Jew even if his or her motives for conversion were dubious, and even if he or she reverts to idolatry after the conversion. Obviously, this would not be an ideal conversion. It is unquestionably preferable to have a convert whose motives are pure, and who lives according to Jewish law ever after. But if a conversion takes place that does not meet the ideal standards, the halakha validates it nevertheless.

Acceptance of Commandments

Although the Talmudic discussions of conversion offer wide latitude in the acceptance of converts, halakhic authorities in the Middle Ages offered more restrictive views. The Tosafot (Ashkenazic sages of the twelfth century) cited *kabbalat ha-mitzvoth* (acceptance of the commandments) as an essential component in

---

[21] *Mishneh Torah*, Isurei Biah 13:17. See also the *Tur* and *Shulhan Arukh*, Yoreh Deah 268.
[22] Yevamot 45b, *mi lo tavla*.

the conversion process.[22] They did not define this term precisely, but it subsequently became part of all halakhic discussions of conversion.[23]

Dr. Zvi Zohar and Dr. Avraham Sagi, in their important studies of conversion, have traced the evolution in the interpretation of the phrase *kabbalat ha-mitzvoth*.[24] Nachmanides (thirteenth-century Spain) understood the term to mean "a commitment of the proselyte, in the presence of the court, to circumcise and to immerse himself."[25] Later rabbinic authorities understood it to mean that the proselyte must make a declaration of a desire to convert, or express a desire to join the Jewish people and religion, or state that he or she understands the norms of the halakha (even if without any intent to observe them in full). In 1876, the notion was posited in some segments of the Ashkenazic world that *kabbalat ha-mitzvoth* requires a commitment on the part of the convert to observe halakha in full, and that the conversion is invalidated if the person

---

[23] The Talmud, Behorot 30b, states that if a non-Jew comes to receive the words of Torah with the exception of one point, we do not receive him. This is sometimes cited to prove that a would-be convert must accept to observe each and every commandment. But it may only mean that we require a general commitment from the candidate for conversion; as long as he does not specifically reject any particular detail, he is accepted. See, for example, Rabbi Benzion Uziel, *Mishpetei Uziel*, vol. 2, Yoreh Deah 58: "If a convert accepts the Torah and the rewards and punishments of the commandments but continues to behave in the way he was accustomed before conversion, he is a sinning convert, but we do not hesitate to accept him because of this." See also Shabbat 31a, where Hillel seemingly accepted converts whose commitment to Torah and mitzvoth had serious reservations. Moreover, the Talmudic description of the conversion process only requires that the convert be informed of some of the light and some of the more serious commandments—not that the convert receive full instruction and accept every detail of the mitzvoth.

[24] *Giyyur ve-Zehut Yehudit*, Shalom Hartman Institute and Mossad Bialik, Jerusalem, 5755; and their article, "The Halakhic Ritual of *Giyyur* and Its Symbolic Meaning," *Journal of Ritual Studies*, 1995, 9:1, pp. 1–13.

[25] Commentary on Yevamot 45b, *mi lo tavla*.

[26] Rabbi Yitzchak Shmelkes, *Beit Yitzchak*, 2:100.

does not observe the mitzvoth following conversion.[26]

The latter view has been increasingly popularized within the Orthodox community. Rabbi Melech Schachter, who for many years taught classes in practical halakha at Yeshiva University's rabbinical seminary, formulated this position as the authoritative one: "Needless to say, conversion to Judaism without commitment to observance has no validity whatever, and the spuriously converted person remains in the eyes of halakha a non-Jew as before."[27]

The differences regarding the meaning of *kabbalat ha-mitzvoth* stem from differences about the nature of conversion. In the classic Talmudic/halakhic view, conversion is the process by which a non-Jew becomes a member of the Jewish people. Indeed, "a non-Jew who has converted is like a newborn child."[28] The convert is then obligated to observe the mitzvoth just as all born Jews are so required. Conversion represents the acceptance of being part of the Jewish people, with all the implications this identity carries.[29] But just as born Jews do not lose their Jewish status by violating halakha, neither do converts lose their Jewish status by transgressing the rules of halakha.

In the restrictive view advanced since 1876, conversion is seen as a total acceptance of all the mitzvoth. Since the mitzvoth are the content and essence of Judaism, no conversion is possible without accepting the mitzvoth in toto. A convert who does not live in full accord with the halakhic lifestyle is therefore not a valid convert.

Conversion involves two distinct aspects: (1) becoming part of

---

[27] See *Jewish Life Magazine*, May–June 1965, p. 7. See also p. 11 under the heading "commitment to total observance." This view was expressed by Rabbi Moshe Feinstein, *Igrot Moshe*, Yoreh Deah 1:157. (But see also Yoreh Deah 1:160, where he states that a conversion performed without proper acceptance of mitzvoth may be valid after the fact.) See also Rabbi Yaakov Breich, *Helkat Yaakov*, no. 13, for a restrictive view.

[28] Yevamot 22a.

[29] If a non-Jew were to accept all the mitzvoth, but not accept being part of the peoplehood of Israel, the conversion would have no validity. See Rabbi Shlomo Goren, *Shanah be-Shanah*, 5743, pp. 149–156.

the Jewish people, and (2) accepting the Jewish religion. The Talmud and the halakhic sources through Maimonides, as well as many subsequent authorities, generally stress the first aspect, assuming that the religious responsibilities naturally flow from one's being part of the Jewish people. The Tosafot and a number of later authorities place greater stress on the religious component, assuming that once a person has accepted the Jewish religion, it follows that he or she becomes part of the Jewish people.

The restrictive view places overwhelming stress on the acceptance of mitzvoth. Perhaps this position came about because there were numerous non-Jews who wished to convert to Judaism but were not committed to full mitzvah observance, or perhaps because of the new availability of non-halakhic conversions in the nineteenth century due to the rise of the Reform movement. By equating Jewishness with mitzvah observance, rabbis hoped to fortify the Orthodox Jewish community.

The restrictive view is quite problematic. First, the halakha recognizes born Jews as Jews whether or not they observe the commandments. There is no equation between being Jewish and observing the commandments. Second, the "full acceptance of all mitzvoth" view flies in the face of the mainstream halakhic precedents in matters of conversion. The classic sources recognized conversions as valid even where there was no clear-cut commitment by the convert to observe each and every mitzvah, and even when the convert violated mitzvoth after conversion.

We have, then, a startling new situation. Suppose a non-Jew converts with circumcision and ritual immersion, is informed of the various commandments as outlined in the Talmud, and has the conversion overseen by a valid Beth Din, but was not fully observant of halakha after the conversion. According to the Talmud, Maimonides, and many other halakhic sources, such a person is Jewish. But for those who advocate the restrictive view, this person is not a convert but remains a non-Jew (i.e., may not marry a Jew and may marry a non-Jew, is allowed to eat non-kosher food, may desecrate the Sabbath, etc.). So the advocates of the restrictive view—in their seeming piety—are actually instructing halakhic converts (as defined by classic halakha) to behave as though they were not Jewish.

A number of halakhic authorities from the nineteenth century and on have, in fact, rejected the restrictive view. While they certainly wanted all converts to observe the mitzvoth in full, they understood that conversions could be valid halakhically even if converts fell short of this desideratum. Professor Shmuel Shilo cites the opinion of a number of sages who permitted conversions even when the would-be convert was not likely to be fully observant of mitzvoth: Rabbis Shelomo Kluger, Shelomo Yehuda of Sighet, Shalom Shvadron, David Zvi Hoffman, Haim Ozer Grodzinski, Yehiel Weinberg, Benzion Uziel, Isser Yehuda Unterman, and Ovadya Yosef.[30]

An analysis of several of the responsa of Rabbi Uziel will be helpful in capturing the complexity of the issues involved. Rabbi Uziel (1880–1953) was one of the great rabbinic leaders of his time, serving as Chief Rabbi of Tel Aviv and Salonika, and then as Chief Rabbi of Israel from 1939 until his death in 1953. A scholar of prodigious erudition, he authored numerous works, including seven volumes of rabbinic responsa entitled *Mishpetei Uziel*.[31]

In 1943, Rabbi Uziel received a halakhic inquiry from Rabbi Hayyim Saban, Chief Rabbi of Istanbul, about the validity of conversions performed for the sake of marriage.[32] Rabbi Uziel noted that intermarriage was increasingly common, and that such mar-

---

[30] The responsa of these sages were discussed by Shmuel Shilo, "Halakhic Leniency in Modern Responsa Regarding Conversion," *Israel Law Review*, 22:3, 1988, pp. 353–364.

[31] See my book *Loving Truth and Peace: The Grand Religious Worldview of Rabbi Benzion Uziel*, Northvale, N.J., Jason Aronson, 1999. Chapter 7 deals with Rabbi Uziel's views on conversion. See also my article "Another Halakhic Approach to Conversions," *Tradition*, Winter–Spring, 1972, pp. 107–113.

[32] *Mishpetei Uziel*, Jerusalem, 5724, no. 18.

riages were readily performed in civil courts. If the non-Jewish partner in such a relationship decides to convert to Judaism, rabbis should perform the conversion. This frees the couple from the sin of intermarriage, and also helps keep their children within the Jewish fold. The rabbis should perform the conversion rather than turn the non-Jewish partner away. The halakha is interested in making it easier for sinners to repent.

Rabbi Uziel believed that the Beth Din must allow the conversion of non-Jewish partners engaged or married to Jews. Rabbis should not take the haughty position that they are wicked people who deserve to suffer the fate of transgressors. On the contrary, by coming to halakhic authorities, the couple thereby displays a desire to be included within the Jewish community.

Rabbi Uziel considered such conversions not only to be permissible, but actually to be morally required. Not only are rabbis allowed to convert a non-Jew for purposes of marriage, but they have a positive responsibility to do so. In support of this view, Rabbi Uziel cited the strict chastisements of the prophet Malakhi against those who married out of the faith: "Yehuda has dealt treacherously, and an abomination is committed in Israel and in Jerusalem; for Yehuda has profaned the holiness of the Lord which He loves, and has married the daughter of a strange god. May the Lord cut off to the man that does this" (Malakhi 2:11–12).

Since intermarriage is such a serious transgression, Rabbi Uziel argued that it was desirable to convert the non-Jewish partner so that the Jewish partner could be spared from this sin. Conversion in these cases is also important to ensure the Jewishness of the children born to such couples. Considering the alternatives of conversion or intermarriage, Rabbi Uziel ruled in favor of conversion.

He qualified his opinion, however, by stating that the rabbis should do such conversions only after concluding that the couple will not agree to break off their relationship. Since they are intent on being married, they should be married as a Jewish couple.

In 1951, Rabbi Uziel dealt with a question sent to him by Rabbi

Yehuda Leon Calfon of Tetuan: "May we convert the non-Jewish wife and children of a Jewish man when we know that he is not observant of the mitzvoth and does not intend to have his family observe the mitzvoth? The man, for example, does not observe Shabbat or festivals according to halakha nor does he keep the laws of kashruth."[33]

In his response, Rabbi Uziel referred to the standard Talmudic/halakhic requirement to inform the would-be convert of some of the easy and difficult commandments, as well as some of the rewards and punishments. We do not tell the person all the technicalities and stringencies. It is clear, then, that there is no requirement to ask the non-Jew to observe the mitzvoth. We do not require his assurances that he will be an observant Jew. If we did, we would never have any converts, because no Beth Din can guarantee absolutely that a convert will observe all the mitzvoth. The conversion procedure requires that we give the potential convert an idea of what is involved in becoming an observant Jew. That way, he has the option to change his mind. If, however, he converts but does not then observe the commandments, he is considered as a Jew who transgresses.

Moreover, informing the would-be convert of Judaism's basic beliefs and commandments is required only initially. If the non-Jew is converted (through circumcision and ritual immersion), the conversion is valid even if he was not informed of the beliefs and commandments.[34]

Rabbi Uziel maintained that a non-Jew who gives no indication that he expects to observe the mitzvoth may still be accepted for conversion even initially. Not only is it permitted to accept converts on this basis, but it is also a positive duty to do so, if this will pre-

---

[33] Ibid., no. 20.

[34] *Shulhan Arukh*, Yoreh Deah 268:12. See also the Gra, no. 28, where he notes that Solomon and Samson remained married to their converted wives even though the wives continued to worship idols.

vent a situation of intermarriage.

Rabbi Uziel believed that turning away potential converts would have negative consequences (e.g., the Jewish partner may abandon Judaism, the rejected convert will have hostile feelings toward Jews and Judaism). Moreover, children of intermarriages are Jewish (if their mother is Jewish) or of Jewish stock (if their father is Jewish), and they are like lost sheep whom we must reclaim for the Jewish people. Rabbi Uziel wrote: "And I fear that if we push them [the children] away completely by not accepting their parents for conversion, we shall be brought to judgment and they shall say to us: You did not bring back those who were driven away, and those who were lost you did not seek" (Yehezkel 34:4).

Another of Rabbi Uziel's responsa deals with a communal ordinance of the Sephardic community in Buenos Aires.[35] The ordinance forbade the acceptance of converts altogether. The policy was adopted as a means of discouraging Jews from dating non-Jews. Knowing that there was no possibility for non-Jews to convert, the Jews would not enter problematic relationships in the first place. A question arose, though, when some rabbis violated this ordinance and converted a non-Jewish woman who planned to marry a Jewish man. Rabbi Uziel was asked whether this conversion was valid. On the one hand, it conformed to the requirements of halakha. On the other hand, it violated a communal ordinance and had been performed without communal authorization.

Rabbi Uziel recognized the right of communities to make ordinances to enhance the religious life of their members, but he was not sure that the ordinance in Buenos Aires was a good idea. He noted that this policy had a stringent aspect

> because we are not to close the door in the faces of those who wish
> to return to the gates of repentance, and to leave them against their
> will in the prohibited relationship and to distance their children

---

[35] *Mishpetei Uziel*, Jerusalem, 5724, no. 13.

[from Jewishness]. . . . It is our obligation to bring them closer to Judaism, not to distance them from the Torah of Israel and from the midst of Judaism forever. I am very much in doubt whether there is in this [ordinance] a [protective] fence for the public, because of which they will avoid intermarriages. Perhaps the opposite [is true]. Since they have no hope of [marrying the non-Jewish person] in a permissible fashion, they will do so in a forbidden manner, and they will drag themselves and their children to leave the Torah of Israel and the community of Israel.

Rabbi Uziel then cited the halakhic sources that would validate conversions even when the convert accepts Judaism for the sake of marriage to a Jewish partner. If, according to halakha, the person is a convert, how could a Beth Din declare him/her to be non-Jewish on the grounds that the conversion violates a communal ordinance? If it does so, the Beth Din would be telling the convert to continue living as a non-Jew, that the laws of the Torah do not apply to him/her, even though the conversion was halakhically valid. Rabbi Uziel stated that if the community wished to maintain its ordinance against conversion, it should at least include some opening whereby a convert might be accepted under special circumstances. He recommended that in the future the community should refer its cases of conversion to the Chief Rabbis in Jerusalem, and let them determine what to do in each situation. This would preserve the intent of the ordinance, but still allow some possibility for converting individuals.

In another responsum, Rabbi Uziel discussed a question relating to a Jewish woman who was married to a non-Jewish man. The husband had agreed to undergo conversion to Judaism. Rabbi Uziel ruled that the couple did not have to wait three months after the conversion before they could marry according to Jewish law. A rabbinic critic of Rabbi Uziel argued that the couple should be compelled to wait the three months usually required by halakha in such cases. "We should not be concerned with their feelings or personal discomfort. After all, they are sinners who intermarried; why should we make life any easier for them?"

Rabbi Uziel responded that God does not want sinners to suffer, but to repent.

> It is incumbent upon us to open the door of repentance; our sages of blessed memory did much for the benefit of those who would repent. Likewise in our case: this woman who wants to free herself from constant sin has brought her non-Jewish husband to convert, and she is bound by his authority. If we say they should separate [for the three-month period], her husband will not listen and will stop from being converted. She will be assimilated among the non-Jews! . . . I admit without embarrassment that my heart is filled with trembling for every Jewish soul that is assimilated among the non-Jews. I feel in myself a duty and mitzvah to open a door to repentance and to save [Jews] from assimilation by [invoking] arguments for leniency. This is the way of Torah, in my humble opinion, and this is what I saw and received from my parents and teachers.[36]

Rabbi Uziel's viewpoint, while lenient in matters of conversion, may also be described as stringent in matters of intermarriage and in concern for keeping children within the Jewish fold. Those who are strict about turning away potential converts are actually letting intermarriages take place or remain intact, and are turning away children from Judaism.

Rabbi Uziel, of course, was not the only rabbinic authority to argue in favor of conversion, even for the sake of marriage and even where the would-be convert was not likely to become a fully observant Jew. His sensitivities and concerns were shared by other sages,

---

[36] *Mishpetei Uziel*, Tel Aviv, 5698, no. 26. For other of Rabbi Uziel's responsa on conversion, see *Mishpetei Uziel*, Jerusalem, 5710, nos. 52, 55, 57, 59, 60, 63, 65, 66.

[37] See, for example, Shelomo Zalman b. Isaac, *Hemdat Shelomo*, Yoreh Deah 29; Shlomo Kluger, *Tuv Taam ve-Daat*, no. 130; David Tzvi Hoffman, *Melamed le-Hoil*, 2: Yoreh Deah 83, 85, 87, 3: 3, 10; Shemuel Matalon, *Avodat Hashem*, E.H. 4; Yehuda Loeb Zirelsohn, *Sefer Atsei ha-Levanon*, Yoreh Deah 63; Eliyahu Hazan, *Taalumot Lev*, 3:29–32; Shalom Messas, *Tevuot Shamesh*, Yoreh Deah 104; David Halevy Horowitz, *Imrei David*, no. 172.

before and since.[37]

Rabbi Haim David Halevy, late Sephardic Chief Rabbi of Tel Aviv, noted that the issue of conversion has long evoked different responses among rabbinic authorities. Some viewed conversion as a moral obligation and a mitzvah; others sought to restrict conversion to the extent possible. These differing tendencies, which were apparent even in Talmudic times, continue to manifest themselves in modern times. Both positions have a legitimate basis: "The rabbinical courts that are lenient in matters of conversion, as well as those that are stringent—their intentions are all for the sake of Heaven, and they work according to their pure understanding and outlook." According to Rabbi Halevy, the Torah specifically omitted reference to a mitzvah of conversion in order to leave the decisions to the rabbinical courts of each generation. There is no one approach which is valid in all places and at all times. Rather, each Beth Din needs to examine every case on an ad hoc basis, trying to reach the correct conclusion based on the immediate circumstances.[38]

This chapter has demonstrated that a variety of legitimate approaches has existed—and does exist—within the halakhic process of conversion. While the restrictive views have grown in influence among Orthodox rabbis of the modern period, the inclusive views have also had thoughtful and authoritative advocates. The spokesmen for the restrictive position tend to be vocal and dogmatic. They actually claim to invalidate conversions that do not meet their specifications. The impression is created among rabbis and laity that the restrictive view is normative; and that those who do not adhere to this view are "compromising" the halakha. As we have seen, however, the lenient authorities, in fact, represent the classic halakhic mainstream, whereas the restrictive ones represent a stringent approach that only took hold among scholars in the late

---

[38] *Asei Lekha Rav*, 1:23. See also 3:29.

nineteenth century.

Since the halakha offers a broad range of opinions as to what constitutes a valid conversion, rabbinic leaders need to have the confidence to judge what is best in each case. Every rabbinic court must operate for the sake of Heaven, and not be intimidated by strident voices of whatever stripe. While rabbis are free to follow the restrictive view if they think it the most correct and appropriate, they are also free to follow more inclusive views if they deem them most correct and appropriate.

Conversion of Children

The conversion of minor children is permitted according to halakha, on the assumption that the parents and the Beth Din are taking responsibility for the conversion. Once a child reaches the age of responsibility (twelve for girls and thirteen for boys), he or she has the right to renounce the conversion and return to the status of a non-Jew, although in actual practice this rarely if ever occurs.

The conversion of children is applicable when a Jewish couple adopts a non-Jewish child or when a Jewish man fathers a child with a non-Jewish woman. Some rabbis have questioned whether it is permissible to convert children when the families in which they will be raised are not religiously observant. They argue that conversion in such cases may in fact be detrimental to the child. Since the child will grow up without learning Torah and mitzvoth, he or she is unlikely to be an observant Jew in adulthood. Thus, instead of being non-Jewish and free from the obligation to do mitzvoth, the child will grow into a Jewish adult who constantly sins by violating the Torah and its commandments.

Against this approach, other rabbis posit that the conversion to Judaism of these children keeps them within the Jewish fold, and helps maintain Jewish families. Moreover, there are many examples of children who grow up in nonobservant Jewish homes who eventually do study Torah and become religiously observant. Rabbi Jack Simcha Cohen, in a thorough analysis of this topic, concluded that conversion of children may be performed "even though the familial milieu lacks observance of commandments."[39] Surely, the Beth Din should do its best to convince the parents of the importance of providing the child with a religious home and education; but ultimately the responsibility is with the parents, not the Beth Din. Each Beth Din must do what it judges best in every given case.

---

[39] Jack S. Cohen, *Intermarriage and Conversion: A Halakhic Solution*, Ktav Publishing House, Hoboken, N.J., 1987, p. 21.

Chapter Five

Issues Faced by Converts

In order to gain a deeper understanding into the phenomenon of conversion, we need to consider some issues faced by the converts themselves. The Talmud states that a person who converts to Judaism is considered as a newborn baby.[40] The convert is the spiritual child of Abraham and Sarah. By joining the people of Israel, the convert has, in some essential way, become a new person with a new identity.

This is a beautiful and powerful rabbinic teaching. If understood literally, though, it can pose some serious dilemmas for converts. If they are now the children of Abraham and Sarah, what is to be their relationship with their biological parents? How are they to relate to their siblings and other family members who are not Jewish? Does their new spiritual identity eclipse or erase their biological roots?

Born Jews do not always appreciate the struggles and sacrifices undergone by converts to Judaism. Converts themselves often are uncomfortable discussing personal issues relating to their biological families. But this is a topic that must be addressed if we are to

---

[40] Yevamot 48b

deal with issues of conversion with greater sensitivity and candor.

The *Shulhan Arukh* records laws relating to the child–parent relationship.[41] The Torah deems it a capital offense to strike or curse one's parents. A question arises: do these laws apply to converts and their biological parents? Technically speaking, since converts are "newborn babies," they no longer have an official child-parent relationship with their biological parents. Nonetheless, the *Shulhan Arukh* rules that converts are not allowed to abuse their biological parents. Indeed, if they were allowed to hit or curse their parents, this would result in a desecration of the Torah. People would say: "When these individuals [the converts] were not Jewish, they were obligated to respect their parents; now that they have accepted Judaism, their new religion allows them to strike or curse their parents!" In order to prevent this calumnious argument, halakha requires that converts demonstrate respect to their parents. Converting to Judaism should never be construed as a way to lessen one's morality and decency.[42]

Converts walk a difficult spiritual tightrope. On the one hand, they must break away from the non-Jewish religious traditions of their biological family; they must enter the peoplehood of Israel by becoming the spiritual children of Abraham and Sarah. This process certainly contains within it the seeds of alienation and separation from family members who adhere to the religious culture in which the convert was raised. On the other hand, converts are expected to maintain proper—even loving—relationships with their biological family members. Aside from the emotional balancing act that this situation may entail, there are also halakhic concerns. For instance, if a convert remains close to the biological family members, might this lead to a forsaking of Judaism and a reversion to the family religion? Might the biological family members put pressure on the

---

[41] Yoreh Deah 241:9.
[42] See Maimonides, Hilkhot Mamrim 5:11.

convert to abandon Judaism?

These concerns are reflected in a number of rabbinic responsa. Rabbi Moshe Feinstein dealt with a question from a female convert to Judaism whose non-Jewish mother was dying.[43] The mother wanted her (now Jewish) daughter to visit her.

It would seem obvious that the daughter should visit her dying mother as an expression of respect and compassion. But isn't there a fear that her mother will influence her to abandon Judaism? She might tell her daughter: "As my last wish to you, please return to your family and your original religious tradition." Even taking these concerns into account, Rabbi Feinstein concluded that the child should heed the mother's request. If the daughter were to say, "No, mother, I cannot visit you now because I am Jewish," this would constitute a desecration of God's name. People would ask, "What kind of religion teaches a child not to visit a dying parent?" The fact is that the mother did give birth to the daughter, raised her, and provided her with education, clothing, and food. A child has a responsibility to show proper respect to someone who has done so much. Even though the child has chosen a Jewish spiritual direction, this does not mean that the biological relationship has been severed. Rabbi Feinstein ruled that the daughter should visit the mother if the mother had specifically asked for her. Indeed, not only should the daughter visit, she must do so; but, of course, she must be very careful not to violate any halakhot during the course of the visit.

Rabbi Haim David Halevy dealt with a related question.[44] A female convert had settled in Israel. Her family lived in the United States. She was invited to attend the wedding of a cousin in the United States—the wedding was to take place in a church. The convert wanted to be part of the family celebration in some way. She felt a closeness to her family and did not want to be alienated from

---

[43] *Iggrot Moshe*, Yoreh Deah 2:130.
[44] *Asei Lekha Rav,* 6:62.

them totally.

Rabbi Halevy ruled that it was not permitted to attend the wedding ceremony in a church. He thought it would be best if she did not go to the United States for the wedding. But if she felt she really wanted to be with her family for this occasion, she could find appropriate ways to be part of her cousin's celebration, as long as she did not violate the strictures of halakha.

Rabbi Ovadya Yosef was asked whether a convert could recite prayers for a non-Jewish parent who is ill, and whether the convert could recite Kaddish if the parent died.[45] Rabbi Yosef noted that it certainly is permissible to visit a sick parent and to recite prayers for the parent's health. Moreover, a convert may recite Kaddish for a deceased non-Jewish parent. The recitation of Kaddish is a sign of respect for the parent because of the parent's vital role in the convert's life. Rabbi Maurice Lamm, in his thoughtful book *Becoming a Jew*, notes that converts may perform all the mourning observances that born Jews do for their parents, such as serving as pallbearers, participating in the burial at the cemetery, and observing the seven-day mourning period.[46]

A delicate situation sometimes arises when a convert marries a born Jew. The convert's parents and siblings are not Jewish; may they participate in the wedding procession? Since the procession itself plays no halakhic role in the wedding, there should be no objection to letting non-Jews walk down the aisle as part of the wedding party. On the other hand, some rabbis feel uneasy about having non-Jews participate in what is, after all, a Jewish religious ceremony. While each case is resolved on the basis of its own inner dynamics, much sensitivity and thoughtfulness are needed to avoid strained feelings. Halakha insists that we not behave in a way that gives the impression that the Jewish religion fosters callousness and

---

[45] *Yehaveh Daat,* 6:60.
[46] Maurice Lamm, *Becoming a Jew*, Jonathan David, Middle Village, N.Y., 1991, pp. 248–249.

bad manners.

Rabbi Maurice Lamm discusses a situation that may arise when a convert becomes the parent of a baby boy. It is an important honor to be invited to hold the baby during the circumcision ceremony. May a non-Jewish relative be invited to hold the baby, that is, serve as sandak? Rabbi Lamm believes the answer is negative, and this seems to be the generally accepted view. Serving as sandak is not merely a ceremonial honor, but carries a specifically religious and spiritual connotation.[47]

Aside from the above issues, converts also may experience inner conflicts when their biological families are celebrating major non-Jewish religious holidays. Should they attend a Christmas party at their parents' home? Should they join in Easter dinner, even if the family provides kosher food? And what about the convert's children? To what extent should they participate in non-Jewish holidays at the homes of their grandparents or their uncles and aunts? Since converts are now Jews, they are bound by Jewish law, which forbids participation in non-Jewish religious holidays and ceremonies. Despite the pain that this may cause, loving families can find alternative ways to spend time together in meaningful ways, without demanding that either Jews or non-Jews compromise on their deeply felt religious beliefs.

Converts may experience internal conflicts at the season of holidays that they joyfully observed before they became Jewish. It takes inner strength and genuine commitment to overcome these nostalgic longings.

While conversion to Judaism entails adjustments in relationships with family members and friends, it also entails adapting to new relationships within the Jewish community. Often enough, converts blend into their Jewish milieu with little trouble. But there are instances where the adjustment to Jewish life is more difficult. Some converts feel that they have not been accepted fully by born

---

[47] Ibid., pp. 256–257.

Jews, that they are still somehow "outsiders." This is particularly painful to them because they have sacrificed so much in order to become Jewish.

The following essays by converts touch on issues relating to their transition into the Jewish community—their ongoing relationships with their families and friends, and their level of acceptance by fellow-Jews. The first is by a man whose spiritual odyssey reflects some of the issues discussed in this chapter.

*   *   *

It took me nineteen years to find my way Home.

Although I have been a Jew all of my adult life, I did not find the fulfillment of my Jewish identity until I was nineteen years old. Coming to that identity and living a Jewish life has been a profoundly gratifying journey of the soul.

I was born into a working-class white Anglo-Saxon family in Suffolk County, New York, and attended a mainstream Protestant church throughout the Eisenhower and Kennedy years. We were regular churchgoers, my brother and I attended Sunday School regularly, and my parents often served on church committees. I was a voracious reader, though, and among other things read much about other religions and traditions. My best friend for many years was Jewish, and I often read whatever English-language texts he studied in Hebrew School.

When I was in my last years of high school, my parents, who had become disaffected with our church, joined an evangelical congregation. They became "born again." I attended with them a few times, but was not attracted. I remember my mother asking me why I did not want to join them. "Why," I asked, "should I go to hear someone tell me that I and all my friends are going to hell?" I did, however, take the time to listen carefully and understand the theological foundations: the evangelicals convinced me that they were absolutely correct in a basic premise; that is, authentic Christianity required one to believe that Jesus died for one's sins and to accept him as the resurrected Christ and one's personal Savior. I knew without doubt or hesitation that this was something I did not, could not, and never would believe.

Thus, I acknowledged for myself that I was not a Christian. In the years since then, I have met many Christians who reject that credo as stated, but nonetheless have a deep faith and profound understanding of the spiritual meaning of the life, person, and symbol of Jesus. I find that I remain unmoved by Christianity's spiritual and symbolic constructs, whether Jesus is central or tangential to them.

Hence, well before I left home for college, I was not a Christian. Still, though, I retained an interest in religion, and in retrospect it is obvious that I had already set foot on my inevitable spiritual path. I do not remember any conscious process of deciding as a freshman to go to the campus Hillel for a class in basic Judaism. As I look back, that seemed as unnecessary as consciously deciding to take my next breath. The class was taught by Rabbi Reuven Kimmelman, and I soon began studying with him toward conversion.

It was a bright new world for me: the exotic mystery of Hebrew and the practical details of kashruth, the soaring inspiration of Zionism and the firm grounding of tradition, the profound intimacy of biblical narrative and the dynamic intellectualism of rabbinic thought. The experience of learning was thrilling, but equally important was the experiential component of my preparation, including services at the traditional minyan and Shabbat at the university's "Kosher Kitchen." Participating with the community in prayer, ritual, and the day-to-day melding of vibrant Jewish life with the realities of a secular world showed me the depth of living what I was studying. Two days before the Shabuoth holiday, I underwent *hatafath dam berith* and mikvah, accepting "the yoke of Heaven's dominion."

Our sages taught that the essential elements of conversion are those which characterized the Israelite experience when the Torah was revealed at Mount Sinai. Just as the Israelites were circumcised, immersed, and voluntarily accepted the obligations of the Torah's commandments, so the convert does. It is a tremendous experience to recapitulate in one's personal life this defining event of the Jewish people.

Sinai, indeed, was a unique event in human history. Unlike other religious traditions, Judaism was not founded on the basis of a single individual's experience or that of a small group, but rather on a revelation to an entire community. A fundamental premise of Jewish understanding of our relationship to God is that the entire people—men, women, and children—were present at this core revelatory experience. The Jewish people thus became what I refer to as an "existential community," by which I mean that it is not simply an aggregation of individuals but was created as a spiritual entity in its own right.

Moses went even further, stating that God had not only entered into a covenantal relationship with the Israelites who came out of Egypt, but with all who would come after them: "I make this covenant, with its sanctions, not with you alone, but both with those who are standing here with us this day before the Lord our God and with those who are not with us here this day" (Deuteronomy 29: 13–14). Our sages explained that the souls of all the Jews who would ever live were also present at the Sinai revelation, including the souls of all sincere converts. Converts, in other words, have Jewish souls; and conversion is simply the process of publicly acknowledging what has always been implicit in one's soul.

After my conversion, I had the great fortune to spend a year studying in Israel at the Pardes Institute. Pardes introduced me to the breadth and depth of Jewish texts and to the thrill of entering into the ongoing conversation with those texts. At Pardes, I was blessed to be exposed to some of the great Jewish thinkers of our time: Rabbi Adin Steinsaltz (editor and translator of Talmud), Professor Michael Rosenak (Hebrew University), Rabbi David

Hartman (Hartman Institute), and Professor Eliezer Schweid (Hebrew University), among others. I am particularly indebted to Mike Rosenak for introducing me to the thought of the great German Jewish existentialist, Franz Rosenzweig.

Perhaps the greatest influence on me was Aryeh Toeg, of blessed memory, a teacher of Bible, soon thereafter martyred in the Yom Kippur War. Aryeh would discuss Wellhausen's theories of biblical source criticism with as much facility as he presented Abraham Ibn Ezra's comments on comparative Semitics. His openness to any honest inquiry that could enhance our understanding and appreciation of the Biblical text was inspiring. I was impressed by his ability to live a committed halakhic life without compromising intellectual integrity, and felt that it was no coincidence that he grew up in a traditional but cosmopolitan Middle Eastern family. At the time, he seemed to me to embody a Sephardi/Middle Eastern worldview which was securely grounded, and therefore not defensive. It seemed to allow for a more confident and open approach to balancing tradition and modernity.

In addition to the joy of studying at Pardes, of course, I had the blessing of living in Israel for almost a year. During the summer, I studied Hebrew in the development town of Arad, still being constructed, where the buildings and streets came to an abrupt stop and I could step off the pavement onto the desert sands of the Negev. At night, after walking across just a few dunes, the city was unseen. Surrounded by the silence and solitude, it was as if no human had stood in that spot ever before. I looked up at the sky and saw the same swath of stars that Abraham had seen when the Almighty showed him how many his progeny would be.

In contrast, I also remember, while walking through the Old City of Jerusalem, looking down at my feet and realizing with awe that the stones I trod were well-worn from the shoes, boots, and sandals of two millennia of human habitation. Somehow that sense of awe at a palpable sense of history rarely experienced by Americans remains with me still, even though I later discovered that the street is many feet above the street level of two millennia ago.

In addition to history, Jerusalem offers a seemingly endless font of prayer experiences, from the majesty of the Kotel (Western Wall) to tiny rooms stuffed with bearded men, inexpensive mystical art, and the fresh fragrance of myrtle leaves. I lived in the Baq'a neighborhood, and although on Saturday mornings we would walk all over the city to explore the variety of synagogues, on Friday nights we generally prayed in a local synagogue. I found both tremendous power and warm comfort in the melodic chants of its Sephardic liturgy.

When I returned to the United States, I decided to continue my Jewish and secular studies in New York. My experiences in my freshman year and in Israel had developed my commitment to traditional Judaism, but I did not feel a need to identify as Orthodox. I did not hesitate to enroll as an undergraduate in a seminary of the Conservative movement. I had the opportunity there to deepen my knowledge, strengthening the philosophical framework I had built at Pardes. At the seminary, and elsewhere in New York, I delighted in the company of others who were actively engaged in exploring the depth and breadth of Jewish learning and in applying to their lives its insights of spirituality, ethics, and the meaning of what it is to be human.

Since arriving in Israel, I had routinely used my Hebrew name, and I continued to do so in New York. Of course, there were circumstances in which I needed to use my legal name, and after a very few years I opted for consistency by changing my name legally. I was happy with my Hebrew name recommended by Rabbi Kimmelman, but I now had to make a conscious choice of last name. The name Obadya resonates in several ways. The Biblical Obadya is the only prophet said by our sages to have been a convert. The definitive ruling which mandated converts to pray the words "God of our ancestors," among other relevant decisions, was issued by Maimonides in a responsum addressed to the convert Obadya. Of course, the literal meaning of the name designates a person who serves and worships the Eternal.

Although changing my name was meant to affirm my identity, it inevitably also pointed out how far away I had grown from my past. No disrespect for my family was intended, but it did emphasize our strained relationship. My conversion had not been welcome to my immediate family. Although my mother was ever-loving, my father stopped speaking to me and refused to see me for fourteen years. My brother could not understand why I would separate myself from them and in so doing hurt my parents so much. Some of my extended family were more accepting, though, and my aunt, uncle, and cousins were important emotional supports. Over years, my father and brother grew more tolerant. Before his death, my father and I developed a closer relationship, and my brother and I now are in touch regularly.

Of course, no matter how enjoyable the times that I spend with my cousins, sister, nephews, and their families, I am not able to share with them the Jewish holidays and the various events of the Jewish life-cycle. Fortunately, I have been welcomed into the lives of many dear Jewish friends over the years, who have generously brought me into their homes to share ritual and other occasions.

In turn, being without Jewish family has encouraged me to provide welcoming opportunities in my own home. A number of friends, some of whom might not have any traditional celebration otherwise, regularly join me for Jewish holidays, and I enjoy creating an atmosphere of tradition and inclusiveness. It is especially gratifying to share with others some of the distinctive traditional Sephardic customs of those occasions. Many Ashkenazic friends have come to treasure the symbolic foods of the Rosh Hashana meal, the table hymn "Bendigamos," and the Passover haroseth of cooked dates and raisins.

Study, synagogue, and home rituals are core components of my life as a Jew, but by its nature our tradition permeates my world throughout the day. When I give charity, whether or not it is for a specific Jewish cause, it is tsedakah. When I eat, the blessings on the food add a taste of tradition. When I shop, kashruth guides my grocery cart. My career provides opportunity for "repairing the world," as I work for a major national nonprofit organization that provides critical human services. My work helps people in need every day, and I am thankful that I can respond to the ethical imperative of my Jewish commitment by applying my professional expertise and experience.

What should be apparent by now is that what I have described of my life as Jew does not differ in any way from the lives of many committed Jews who happened to have been born into Jewish families. The conversion experience does not separate me from my community, but was intended to assure a complete integration into the community. Hence, I tend not to identify myself as a "Jew by Choice," in part because I am not sure how much choice I had on a cosmic level, and in part because I do not really see how that identification is useful. When the subject comes up (often because I am asked about the origins of my "family" name), I simply explain that my family is not Jewish. I have found that this provides the essential information in the most neutral way. I am not ashamed or embarrassed by the fact of my conversion, but neither do I consider it special or any particular reason for pride.

I underwent an Orthodox conversion, I belong to two Orthodox synagogues, and I believe that halakha as a process is the best way for our tradition to progress. Yet I also believe that Orthodoxy is not sufficiently inclusive or welcoming. Indeed, Orthodoxy in our time has too often failed its sons and daughters by lacking the courage of past generations to utilize the halakhic process to make changes necessary to do what is right.

What matters to me is the Truth of Torah, not in the sense of historical details, but the path it provides to what matters most, to the eternal meanings of our experience, to the Divine infinite. It is that Truth which has guided my soul's journey.

In the sense that Torah offers its Truth without limitations of time or place, I can say that the souls of all Jews, past, present and future, were at Mount Sinai to experience divine revelation. Indeed, in that sense I can personally attest to the Truth of our existential community experience at Sinai.

I was there.

*   *   *

The following essay, written by a female convert, reflects the frustration felt by some converts with their integration into the Jewish community.

I grew up in Europe in a religiously devoted Catholic family. For our family, Catholicism certainly governed every thought and, by extension, most deeds. For me, some form of real engagement with religious life was essential. If I could not function fully within the Catholic community, I needed to find one in which I could.

My choice of Judaism, as a young adult, was largely the result of an intellectual journey. Arriving at college, I finally had the freedom to break from the practice of Catholicism. I also had access to the resources I needed to pursue a serious study of the theological issues which troubled me. Ironically, during this period I lived at the Catholic chaplaincy and was supported through my search by a Dominican. At the end of three years, I had collected a degree but had reached no real conclusion to my religious search. I was no longer a Catholic, but I wasn't anything else either.

It was actually through contact with the Dominicans that I became friendly with a number of non-Orthodox rabbis with whom I began to study Biblical texts. Every month, I attended an informal study group. Slowly, I moved toward a more mainstream community setting, attending a non-Orthodox synagogue. I became involved in the Hillel at the local university and began babysitting for a Sephardic Jewish family in return for Hebrew lessons. It was with this family that I learned to prepare for Passover with a thoroughness that I suspect now drives my husband to distraction. This was also where the subject of conversion first arose. The husband suggested that I take the Orthodox route. I wasn't sure I could keep all the rules. I approached the rabbi of the non-Orthodox synagogue, he, too, suggested that I consider Orthodoxy. But I still wasn't sure this would be right for me.

Shortly after, I moved to another city for employment, and I did not immediately approach another rabbi. I did, though, find an agreeable synagogue and became active in a young adult group. I attended services and social gatherings, helped arrange lectures, and became involved in community projects. I felt no urgency to take the final steps of conversion. I left for a year to train as a teacher, during which time I attended an Orthodox synagogue. The rabbi welcomed me into his small community. His wife suggested that I travel to Israel. She let me know that the local Orthodox Beth Din was not accepting of converts. After I completed my training, I returned home, and took stock of my situation.

Though active and completely comfortable within my community, there were certain things I could not do, since I had not yet converted to Judaism. I could not become a member of the synagogue, nor teach in its Hebrew School, nor marry and raise a Jewish family. Indeed, if I were to die suddenly, I would not have qualified to be buried in a Jewish cemetery. I decided to present myself for instruction as a candidate for conversion; by the end of the year I was approved by the non-Orthodox Beth Din, and went to the mikvah.

The non-Orthodox rabbis reminded me that the conversion would not be accepted by the Orthodox and that making aliyah to Israel might also be problematic. These concerns did not trouble me at the time. I was a full member of my community, a teacher in the Hebrew School, and active in the more traditional faction of the community. We kept kashruth, and avoided unnecessary travel on Shabbat. A group of us met monthly in members' homes for services and lunch. We wanted to return to the traditional liturgy and full Torah reading, and to come to grips with texts and concepts that were not part of the Reform Jewish experience. I began to consider the possibility of an Orthodox conversion—the gap between where I was and where I needed to be did not seem so great anymore.

Meanwhile, I had obtained a partial scholarship to study for a master's degree in Jewish education in the United States in a Conservative Jewish institution. I learned there that my previous Reform conversion was not valid due to a technicality, and so I underwent conversion again under Conservative auspices.

I began to realize, though, that barriers did exist between converts and born Jews. Perhaps I had been extraordinarily lucky at home, but I had never been made to feel bothered by the fact that I was a convert. Now, though, I was facing some unpleasant situations. A fellow student informed me that my family name was very "Waspy." At a party, a conversation came to an abrupt end when it emerged that I was not a born Jew. Whereas my conversion had been a religious journey for me, I now saw that blood lines and ethnicity had become an issue.

I returned home for the summer, by which time I was no longer traveling or turning electricity on or off on Shabbat. Further transformations occurred the following year when I stood in for a friend as a volunteer chaplain in a nursing home. I applied and was accepted in rabbinical school and in a doctoral program. I set out with the intention of becoming a hospital chaplain and an educator, and I followed up my previous experience with a year's internship in hospice. I took extra courses in psychology and counseling and began to suspect I might be happier as a social worker or therapist.

Finally, during a year off from rabbinical school, I began with a friend to go to services at several Orthodox synagogues. I found I enjoyed the services and was not bothered by the lack of public participation in the liturgy by women. During the course of a year, I realized that "keeping the rules" was no longer an obstacle. I decided to take the final step to become fully part of the Jewish community. I left rabbinical school, and chose to live according to Orthodox Judaism. I converted again under the auspices of an Orthodox Beth Din.

I have a full life within my own Orthodox synagogue community, including participation in women's services. I have also gained much from friendships within the haredi community.

It must be noted, though, that there has been a definite change in the feeling of openness that I had after the original conversion. I have learned that it is wise to hide my background where possible. It is not just the prejudice I sometimes have felt from individuals; it is also the institutionalized opposition to conversion maintained by a certain community in whose midst my husband and I live. I have begun to wonder if being a convert carries a stigma in other Jewish communities as well.

It is sad that the most momentous choice of my life is something I do not feel able to rejoice in openly.

* * *

The following essay, by a male convert with distant Jewish ancestry, sheds light on the adaptation problems faced by some converts. The author of this essay is actively involved in Jewish life both personally and professionally. Nevertheless, he still feels somewhat like an "outsider."

"You just don't understand! You're not Jewish!" Such was my introduction to Judaism, my first major rejection as an outsider, and the feelings of alienation that my position brought with it.

The comment did not mean much to me at the time. I knew very little about Jews, and I knew even less about my own Jewish connections. I was on what had been advertised as an "Archaeological Seminar," and was intent on studying archaeology in Israel. I had no idea that the trip, sponsored by the American Zionist Youth

Federation, was actually designed to convince young Jews of the desirability of living in Israel. I returned from Israel feeling a bit dispirited and alienated: an identity crisis?

Little did I expect that shortly after my return, my grandmother on my father's side (a professional genealogist) would unearth evidence that my mother's father came from a long line of rabbis, cantors, and Jewish scholars. This set me on the road to recovering my lost Jewish identity. A Hebrew professor once told me that there were only two reasons for converting to Judaism: either one felt a burning in the gut, or one felt that he had a heritage that had been lost. I felt that I had a heritage that had been lost. Yet, although I felt that I was motivated by the latter reason, it appeared (and often still appears) that neither was entirely satisfactory to the Jews around me. No matter what I have done to gain acceptance as a Jew, I continue to feel like an outsider.

My first steps toward Judaism were kind of wobbly and marred by feelings of rejection. When I suggested to Jewish acquaintances that I was part Jewish, and that I would have been persecuted as a Jew during the Holocaust, they would have none of it. I was met with flat rejection. "You're either Jewish or you're not," they said, "and if you're mother wasn't Jewish, you're not Jewish."

I began by taking Hebrew classes at the local Jewish community center, but the people running the classes were secular Israelis who had little interest in introducing me to religious beliefs and observances. Then one summer, I encountered two stimuli which set me on the road to conversion: I met a woman who was interested in conversion, and I met a co-worker who had already undergone a Conservative conversion. The new girlfriend provided the impetus, and the co-worker provided an entrance to the world of the Conservative synagogue. My co-worker and her husband drove my girlfriend and me to services one Friday night, and that marked the beginning of my personal involvement in Jewish religious life.

I began attending services regularly on Shabbat, I began speaking with rabbis, and most of all I read. I read Jewish history, Jewish philosophy, even Jewish fiction. Indeed, I made it a policy only to read books with Jewish content of some kind. I knew I had to focus my efforts. Within a few years, I had convinced the Conservative rabbis that I was ready for conversion. I went before the local Beth Din and was readily accepted into the fold. What I could not understand, though, was why I had to explain my observance of the laws of kashruth to this group of elders. The laws seemed so intrinsic to being a Jew that I couldn't conceive of myself living any other way. Yet here arose one of the dilemmas that was forever to confuse me: how was it that those who had been born as Jews could neglect or even reject the mitzvoth and still be endorsed as good Jews, when the convert was expected to uphold and adhere to the same mitzvoth or face rejection as a hypocrite and a non-genuine convert? That was a question a bit further down the road for me, however, since this first Beth Din expected very little in the way of religious observance. Even so, I could see right then and there that this issue of observance would sooner or later prove a problem that would haunt me in the future.

I was immediately dissatisfied with this so-called conversion. There was no circumcision, no mikvah, and no acceptance in Israel. I was well aware, right from the start, that an Orthodox conversion was necessary for recognition in Israel, and I had every intention of returning to Israel. Living in my rural, mid-western community, I somehow knew that I would need to find acceptance before an Orthodox Beth Din. The next step was to find an Orthodox rabbi in a nearby urban community who would arrange to carry out the necessary procedures. This, then, is what I did—I found an Orthodox rabbi, and he called in two older men who were Sabbath observers to form a Beth Din. But the process seemed mechanical rather than spiritual. I flew in to the town; they observed the drop of blood of the symbolic circumcision (*hatafat dam berit*), the immersion in the mikvah, and they signed the certificate. They did not ask me any questions, and were not impressed by the fact that I came from a long line of conversos and rabbis. Afterwards, they couldn't even recommend a kasher place for me to eat.

Did I feel different after this second conversion? Not particularly. On the contrary, I was now embarrassed by my status, and found myself desperately striving for acknowledgement and acceptance, while the many Jews around me couldn't care less about my inner struggles. The only solace I could find was in learning about my long and extensive Jewish family heritage. But this heightened my frustration because I felt disconnected from the Jewish people of my own time. Unlike other converts I know, I took no pride in my conversion. I felt that I had already really been Jewish—that my thoughts, my heritage, my whole being was Jewish.

And then there were feelings of guilt. Since I had assumed the obligation of the mitzvoth, I felt that I was obliged to fulfill them to the best of my ability. Yet I lived miles away from the nearest synagogue and would have had to drive there to attend on Shabbat. This was a real dilemma for me: should I drive to the synagogue on Shabbat in violation of halakha, or should I stay home alone on Shabbat?

I decided to find out more about Judaism by attending a baal teshuva yeshiva in Jerusalem. This would provide the opportunity to study Talmud and other classic texts. Baal teshuva yeshivot were established to help beginners and returnees to Judaism, striving to give them text skills as well as an Orthodox mindset. My experience, though, was very negative. It seemed to me that these institutions strove to destroy their students' faith in science and secular authority, and to replace it with a new faith—narrowly conceived—in God and Torah. Rather than learning to love one's neighbor, students sometimes came to feel hostility to those less observant of Torah, or to condemn science and scientists. I certainly did not share this view. I had been a student of science and history for a long time, and I was not readily convinced that the Torah disproved Darwin's theories. (Many years later, I was happy to find support for the theory of evolution in the writings of a prominent Orthodox rabbi, Dr. David de Sola Pool, in an article he had written for the

Jewish Forum in April 1926.)

An additional frustration confronted me. It seemed that the baal teshuva individual never seemed to be accepted completely by those who were religious from birth. Yes, it was good that we had extricated ourselves from the quagmire of more liberal Jewish movements; but we never seemed to be as knowledgeable and comfortable religiously as those who had been religious all their lives.

After my stay in Israel, I went to New York, where I decided to undergo yet a third conversion procedure. This time I studied seriously and appeared before a Beth Din of three Orthodox rabbis. I worked at Talmudic texts, upgraded my level of knowledge and observance, and attended daily prayer services. At last I succeeded in becoming a fully halakhic convert, although I still have issues with my spiritual life. In spite of my faithfulness in daily prayer, I rarely get a sense of genuine communication between myself and God. But I am working on this, and hope to grow in my prayer experience.

I keenly feel that I have adopted Judaism to reconnect with my ancestors' faith, and I truly want to do this in the fullest sense possible. But it is for this very reason that I feel so desperate in my striving. I feel like an eternal outsider, trying with all my might to gain readmission to a club that doesn't quite know what to make of me. I would think that these feelings were just my own perceptions deceiving me, and yet I am aware of certain groups and individuals who clearly exclude or demean converts. I wish they would take some time to reflect on the Torah's commandment to love the convert, and try to understand how their rejectionism causes so much pain to those striving to follow the ways of God. Meanwhile, I continue to strive to improve myself and to prove my Jewishness.

Chapter Six

Conversion for Those of Jewish Ancestry

In the preceding essay, the author wrote that he had discovered his Jewish ancestry through the genealogical research of a relative. Having Jewish roots was a strong impetus in the decision to convert. In a sense, he was recovering the Jewish heritage that had been forcibly ripped away from his family due to the religious fanaticism in medieval Iberia.

In recent years, there has been a resurgence of interest in Judaism on the part of "crypto-Jews"—descendants of Jews who, under duress, were converted to Catholicism in medieval Spain and Portugal. Many of the forced converts were absorbed into the Catholic community, but others maintained a secret Jewish identity and continued to practice some Jewish rites. Conversos suspected of Judaizing, though, were subject to the immense cruelty of the Spanish and Portuguese Inquisitions. So it was far from a simple matter to transmit Jewish identity and practices from generation to generation.

During the sixteenth and seventeenth centuries, some crypto-Jews managed to leave the Iberian Peninsula and settled in lands where they could rejoin the Jewish people and practice their religion openly. Amsterdam became a hub for returning conversos. Ex-converso Jewish communities emerged in such places as Paris, Bordeaux, Bayonne, Hamburg, and London, as well as in the New

World.

While these individuals left their crypto-Judaism behind them to embrace Judaism openly, other conversos continued to live as crypto-Jews. Some settled in the New World in the hope that they could escape the grasp of the Inquisition. But the Inquisition crossed the Atlantic Ocean with them.

That any sort of Jewish identity could have survived among descendants of conversos must be counted as one of the amazing phenomena in the history of religion. For centuries, they lived under the shadow of the Inquisition. They had little or no contact with actual Jewish communities, and did not have access to authoritative teachers of Judaism. Nonetheless, some families did manage to transmit traditions of Jewishness through the generations, in spite of the difficulties and dangers. Some of those who have returned to Judaism have said: "The blood calls." They feel that their Jewish "blood"— their genetic tie to Jewish ancestors—was somehow a driving force in their decision to "come back home" to the religion of their ancestors.

A striking case in point is the community in Belmonte, Portugal, which functioned for nearly five centuries as a crypto-Jewish entity. Outwardly, the people were Catholic. Yet they managed to maintain various rites and prayers that kept them aware of their Jewish antecedents. In recent years, members of this community have openly reclaimed their Jewish heritage, and the community in Belmonte now operates as a Jewish community.[48]

In Spain and Portugal, as well as in Latin America and the American Southwest, individuals have been discovering their Jewish roots. In some cases, they had long had a vague awareness of their Jewish past. In other cases, they were oblivious of their Jewish roots,

---

[48] The fascinating story of the Belmonte community is recorded in *The Last Crypto-Jews of Portugal*, by David Augusto Canelo, translated by Werner Talmon-l'Armee, IJS, Portland, Or., 1990.

but became aware of them through study and genealogical research.

Over the years, quite a few individuals with Spanish and Portuguese Jewish ancestry have found their way to me. Some wanted to convert to Judaism, to rejoin the people of their ancestors. Others wanted to learn more about the Sephardic experience, without any actual intention of becoming Jewish. Yet others have wanted to be accepted as Jews without need of conversion, in light of the fact that they had Jewish ancestors. Each of these individuals has been a source of enlightenment to me, opening up another dimension of the Jewish spiritual heritage.

The following letter was written to me by a man who discovered his Jewish roots. The letter is a poignant example of the desire to return to Judaism among some of those who have Jewish ancestors.

*   *   *

My name is ——, and I want to know if you can help me; but first I will tell you my story. I was born in the Dominican Republic. About four years ago, I came to the United States and here I became interested in Judaism. I don't know why, but even though I did not know or hear about Jews in my country, I was attracted to everything Jewish.

In 1995 I started to attend a Conservative synagogue in New York, where I began the process of conversion. Then I moved to Boston, where I finished the process under Conservative auspices. But before I moved to Boston, one day I was reading the *Jewish Encyclopedia* and saw a converso's surname which was the same as mine. I was very confused about my surname and how a Jewish man had been named with it.

I started a family tree and I sent money to my father in the island. He went to the church of the town, and then the Catholic priest sent my father to a historian who lives in the same town. He told my father that my family descends from a converso's family in Spain. The historian went to the main church in the Republic and found that 250 years ago, my great-, great-, great-, great-, great-grandfather left Andalusia, a region in the south of Spain.

I am very confused about my history and my ancestors' adoption of Christianity 608 years ago. I have restarted the conversion process with an Orthodox Beth Din. As a member of the —— family, and you being a Sephardic rabbi, please forgive what my family did 608 years ago. It is very important for me to feel this forgiveness.

In responding to his letter, I said: "The story of your return to Judaism is very moving, and I wish you much happiness within the community of the Jewish people. In the Jewish tradition, each individual is judged on his own deeds, and is not held responsible for actions taken by ancestors. You have no reason to feel guilt about what happened over six centuries ago. On the contrary, you should be proud that you have found your way back to your original people."

Another letter to me sheds further light on the interest in Judaism of those of converso background.

* * *

Dear Rabino,

It is not easy to make the decision to contact you. It comes after a process of discovery of my "crypto-Jewish" roots as a journalist who worked in New York for radio and television. 90 percent of my family live in Sefarad [Spain]. I discovered my Jewish roots in 1992 when I covered the events of the 500th anniversary [of the expulsion of Jews from Spain] in Andalusia.

I returned to New York very depressed, and I talked to my mother and father [about our family's Jewish antecedents]. My mother sent me to see an older uncle in Uruguay. He told me that our family left Sefarad in 1492 from the Navarra region, settled in Portugal, and then fled to the Azores Islands. From there, they fled to Brazil to Viamao. . . . My father refused to talk about this and had promised my grandfather never to say a word; he kept his promise to his death. But my mother and an aunt explained to me the family secret. . . . I am asking for your help to convert to Judaism. The names on my mother's side of the family are [names of Sephardic Jewish families].

The following is an excerpt from a letter to me from a woman of converso background who converted back to Judaism. She became an active member of the Jewish community in a city in Texas.

*   *   *

"The story of the *anusim* [forced converts and their descendants] is a powerful story of survival, courage, strength, and hope. We have not disappeared, nor will we. I can vouch for how much courage and strength it takes to return. We are going to return to Judaism, nothing and no one will prevent that, especially when it is Hashem who destines it. When will it be? How many will it be? Only Hashem knows. The rabbinical community needs to prepare to handle the return of *anusim*, in large or small numbers."

In the spring of 1995, I traveled to New Mexico and Colorado, where I met with individuals and groups who believe themselves to be descendants of conversos. Dr. Stanley Hordes, of the Latin American Institute at the University of New Mexico, was kind enough to arrange for these meetings, so that I, as an Orthodox Sephardic rabbi, could hear directly from those who were in the process of rediscovering and reconnecting with their Jewish roots. I met with the leaders of crypto-Jewish societies in Santa Fe and Denver, as well as with individuals who had come from as far away

---

[49] In Denver, a meeting was held in the home of Dr. and Mrs. David Kazzaz. Dr. Kazzaz also arranged for me to give a public lecture, which drew a large audience, many of whom spoke to me of their Jewish roots. Dr. Kazzaz is founder of the Hispano-Crypto-Jewish Resource Center in Denver. During my trip to New Mexico and Colorado, I had the opportunity to meet individually or in groups with several hundred people of crypto-Jewish background.

as Texas and California for these meetings.[49]

Some of these individuals had done considerable genealogical research and could verify their Jewish ancestry. Some had family traditions of their Jewish roots. Yet others grew up unaware of their Jewish heritage, but discovered it later in life when they learned about crypto-Jewish history and traditions. Some pointed to family surnames that were typical of Sephardic Jews. Others remembered family practices and rituals that suggested Jewish origins: abstinence from pork, circumcision of boys, drinking wine and breaking a glass at weddings, bathing and changing linens on Fridays, washing blood off meat before cooking it, sitting on the floor while mourning the death of a near relative.

There was a palpable desire among many of the group to be considered members of the Jewish community. Quite a few, however, were glad to know of their Jewish past but did not wish to adopt the Jewish religion. Some of them had undergone conversions to Judaism, while others thought that their Jewishness was adequately proven by their genealogical research and family traditions.

The halakhic status of these converso descendants is a matter of painful controversy. Since they grew up without a public Jewish identity, and since their ancestors did not live openly as Jews for many generations, it is almost impossible to "prove" their Jewish status according to halakha. Nevertheless, these individuals do have a claim of Jewishness that must not be ignored.

I sent the following letter to an Orthodox rabbi who asked me about the Jewishness of a member of his community who believed herself to be of Jewish ancestry.

Dear Rabbi ——

Thanks for your recent telephone call and letter concerning Mrs. ——, who wishes to convert to Judaism according to halakha. You informed me that she had undergone a Conservative conversion fifteen years ago, and that her children were not accepted as students in the Orthodox Jewish Day School because they were not Jewish according to (Orthodox) halakha. You also informed me that her mother, of Hispanic background, has long observed various Jewish practices, e.g., lighting candles on Friday night. You raised the question of whether or not Mrs. ——— might actually be Jewish, a descendant of crypto-Jews of Sephardic background.

Although it is possible that she and others in her situation are in fact of Jewish ancestry, it is usually not possible to prove this Jewishness. Who has accurate records, generation to generation on the maternal side, that can definitely tie one to a Jewish ancestor without any doubt?

Where we have a plausible reason to assume that a person may well be of Jewish ancestry, it seems to me that we need to make every effort to bring him/her into the Jewish fold by means of a conversion from doubt. In the eyes of God, this person may very well be Jewish: so if we turn her away and don't let her educate her children in a day school, then we may be guilty of turning Jewish souls away from Torah. We simply cannot treat Mrs. ——— (or others in her situation) as being non-Jewish. There is a possibility, and a reasonable one, that she is really Jewish and should be observing the mitzvoth as a proper Jew. We should be helping her in this direction.

In 1995, the Sephardic Chief Rabbi of Israel, Rav Mordecai Eliyahu, ruled that such individuals should be converted to Judaism *misafek* [from doubt that they might really be Jewish]. He suggested that the certificate given to them on the occasion of their immersion in the mikvah should not be captioned as a conversion certificate, but rather as a certificate "for one who has returned to the ways of his/her ancestors."[50]

My suggestion to you in the case of Mrs. ——— is to encourage a conversion *misafek* as early as is feasible, on the possibility that she may in fact be Jewish. Each day of delay is keeping her

---

[50] The letter is dated 1 Ellul 5755. Rabbi Eliyahu wrote that such individuals should be praised for coming to observe the mitzvoth openly. The certificate should be captioned: *Te-udah le-shav le-darkhei avotav*, certificate for one who has returned to the ways of his/her ancestors.

and her family outside of the Jewish people when they really belong inside the Jewish people. The certificate should be captioned according to the suggestion of Rav Mordecai Eliyahu. Her children (who should also be converted *misafek*) should be enrolled in a Jewish day school as soon as possible. May this family become a source of strength and blessing to the entire Jewish people.

Those of converso background who wish to reclaim their Jewish heritage should be encouraged to undergo halakhic conversion to ensure their acceptance as Jews within the overall Jewish community. Even if they think themselves to be Jewish already, the conversion process eliminates halakhic problems for them and their children. Orthodox rabbis should be especially receptive to helping such individuals rejoin the Jewish people.

Aside from individuals of converso background, there are also others whose Jewish ancestry has inspired them to seek halakhic conversion to Judaism. Some years ago, three individuals approached me about their interest in converting to Judaism. They were originally from Turkey, and were part of a group known in Turkish as Dönmeh. Their ancestors in the seventeenth century were Turkish Jews who believed that Sabbatai Sevi was the messiah. In 1666, Sevi converted to Islam rather than be executed by the sultan. While this act of apostasy convinced the masses of Jews that Sabbatai Sevi was merely an imposter, a pseudo-messiah, some of his followers did not lose faith in his messianic claims. They actually converted to Islam in emulation of Sabbatai Sevi. They thought that the apostasy was just a temporary measure that would soon give way to a great redemption for the Jewish people. When Sabbatai Sevi died in 1676 without having redeemed the Jews, many of these converts realized that he was a false messiah and returned to their Jewish lives. Yet some of Sevi's staunchest supporters persisted in their belief that he was messiah; they claimed that he would return from death and fulfill his mission as messiah.

This latter group continued to live as Muslims, although they believed in a Jewish messiah—Sabbatai Sevi—who would someday return to redeem the Jewish people, of whom they knew they were part. They maintained many Jewish practices, and spoke Judeo-Spanish into the latter part of the nineteenth century. They came to be known as Dönmeh ("converts, apostates"). In recent years, a number of people of Dönmeh background have chosen to identify openly as Jews. Some have undergone halakhic conversions. Others are demanding to be acknowledged as Jews based on the fact that the Dönmeh historically maintained themselves as a separate group and generally married only within their sect. Yet others, especially those still living in Turkey, are troubled by public discussion of their Jewish antecedents, since they feel this may compromise their status in the overwhelmingly Muslim population.

It was a source of great personal satisfaction for me to arrange for the instruction and conversion of the three individuals of Dönmeh background. It was like retrieving lost sheep into the fold. Their ancestors had been cut off from normative Jewish life for centuries, but the spark of Jewishness was able to transcend time and be rekindled in our generation. These three individuals now live intensely Jewish lives, study Torah and observe mitzvoth, and are glad that they have rejoined the Jewish people.

Another group of converts is made up of people whose discovery of a Jewish ancestor inspired them to study Judaism and Jewish history. I personally have dealt with a number of candidates for conversion who were raised as Christians and whose ancestors had been Christians for generations. The last of their Jewish ancestors had abandoned Judaism, either accepting Christianity or marrying a Christian spouse. Now the descendants sought to rejoin the community of Jews which their ancestor had abandoned. They wanted to undo their ancestor's decision to cut off the family's Jewish line and to reestablish its identity within the Jewish people.

A number of candidates for conversion are children of Jewish fathers and non-Jewish mothers. Since the halakha defines Jewishness according to the mother's line, such children are technically not Jewish. Some of them grow up in non-Orthodox communities and feel themselves to be Jewish. Others have been raised without a religion or in a non-Jewish religious tradition—they have little or no Jewish identity, but still recognize a Jewish component to their lives. Since these individuals already have at least some ethnic feeling of being connected to the Jewish people, their transition into Judaism is often fairly smooth.

Over the years, I have dealt with quite a few individuals who thought themselves to be Jewish but were not Jewish according to halakha. This group includes those with a Jewish father and a non-Jewish mother, but also those whose mother (or even grandmother) had been converted under non-halakhic auspices. In many cases, these individuals have grown up with a definite Jewish identity and are stunned to learn that they are not Jewish by halakhic standards. I have explained to them that they certainly do have a Jewish identity, and do feel part of the Jewish people. Due to technical problems with the conversion of their mother/grandmother, the halakhic standards for Jewishness have not been met. In most cases, a calm and reassuring explanation has helped them to understand their situation, and in many cases such individuals have opted to undergo halakhic conversion.

Another category of converts includes those who do not seem to have any Jewish ancestry, yet feel that they have "Jewish souls." A rabbinic teaching has it that all the souls of the Jewish people were present at Mount Sinai when God gave the Israelites the Ten Commandments. The souls of everyone who would eventually convert to Judaism were also at Sinai. Some people, born non-Jewish, sense an almost mystical connection to Judaism, as though their souls were indeed at Sinai.

*   *   *

The following essay was written by a woman, herself a grandmother, who underwent a halakhic conversion although she had felt herself Jewish all her life.

As early as I can remember, I felt in my heart that I was Jewish. This is significant, since my mother was of another faith. Let me introduce you to my parents and tell you of my background.

My father was born of observant Jewish parents of Russian heritage, and raised in a very modest home on the Lower East Side of Manhattan. He cherished memories of learning Torah, especially from his immigrant grandfather. When I was growing up, I recall that he looked forward every week to attending Shabbat services with my mother and enjoyed participating in the discussions that were held after services.

My mother was raised in the university town of Charlottesville, Virginia, born of educated Christian parents whose ancestors were among the earliest settlers of our country. She met my father when she was only sixteen years old. As a young accountant, he had occasion to travel to Virginia on an assignment. Several years later, before marriage, she accepted a position as a nurse-in-training at Mount Sinai Hospital in New York, which also enabled her to learn more about the Jewish faith and about life in New York City.

Not until recently did I discover a letter written by my father to my mother saying that he loved her very much and, as she knew, wanted to marry her; but that he could not bring himself to raise his children in any other religion than Judaism. Would she think about his proposal carefully, given the seriousness of the decision, and let him know her answer. Shortly after, they were married in New York City.

As agreed, my sister and I, from birth, were raised in the Jewish faith. My parents joined a Reform temple. Both my mother and father attended Friday night services frequently and also enjoyed socializing with friends. My sister and I attended classes at the temple every Sunday from grade school through high school. I was a member of the high school confirmation class. I especially looked forward to the class taught by our rabbi. It was there that I loved studying the Ethics of the Fathers. My original classroom book still sits today on a shelf in my family room.

Our neighborhood was 90 percent Jewish, a mix of Reform, Conservative, and Orthodox. In my grade school, an unusual but short-lived program was established where children, with the written permission of parents, were excused for religious training. I accompanied the other Jewish children to the small Orthodox synagogue just down the block from my home. That was my first exposure to Orthodox Judaism, however brief. I was also, along with many of my friends, a member of a Young Judea group during my grade school years. We met in a classroom in an Orthodox synagogue. I still remember with fondness some of the Hebrew songs we learned at that time.

Of course, there were difficulties. On occasion, while always feeling loved and very close to my mother, I felt much compassion for her when she often went by herself to her church services in a nearby town. She, however, seemed satisfied, having made many friends there.

Both of my parents always said that, although they had a mixed marriage, they preferred that we marry in the Jewish tradition in which we had been raised. It was their opinion that it was much easier to raise children when the partners are of the same religion. In choosing social relationships, they naturally gravitated toward persons whose outlook was one of friendship and understanding, and not those who demonstrated any form of unpleasant prejudice or lack of tolerance toward those who were not of their tradition.

When I was of dating age, my parents encouraged me to wear my Magen David necklace, so that Jewish young men would know of my heritage. Of course, living in my neighborhood, most of my social contacts were Jewish in any event.

And so I thought my identity was established and secure. Or

was it?

My husband and I met in my hometown. He was the brother of one of my Jewish friends. I accepted when he proposed, and we happily prepared for our wedding day. We were to be married by a Conservative rabbi of a nearby synagogue, since my rabbi had a prior commitment on our chosen day, and my synagogue had already been reserved for another wedding. One day I received a call from the rabbi who was to officiate at our wedding. He needed to talk to me before our ceremony.

I met him in his study, when he told me that he had just learned that my mother had not converted, and that he thought it best that I convert before the wedding. Convert? Convert? I was already Jewish! Why should I convert to a religion that I already cherished? He explained to me that according to Jewish law I needed to convert. Tears rolled down my cheeks. Here is the gist of what I said to him: You are asking me to convert to Judaism. To do that, you must take away my cherished Jewish identity, just to give it back to me after a mikvah ceremony. It would be the same as taking away my mother or father from me and telling me I am an orphan who needs to be adopted. Can you imagine how that feels? My identity was challenged and would never be the same. How can you give me what is already mine? I will not go to the mikvah to become someone I already am!

Well, I certainly gave the rabbi a challenge. He then asked me questions about Judaism, about the holidays, beliefs, customs, and so forth. I answered everything correctly. After a long pause, a thoughtful look appeared on his face. Suddenly, he raised his hand up high, brought it down hard on his desk to emphasize his remarks, and said: "I will marry you."

On a memorable June day, we were married by this Conservative rabbi. It is now forty-two years later. We have raised three wonderful children. The Orthodox tradition was chosen by my son, who also chose to be converted because of his grandmother not being Jewish. One daughter is Reform, and the other, having married a Conservative Jewish husband, usually attends Conservative synagogue services.

When the children were in grade school, I became very involved in several Jewish organizations. I am a life member of Hadassah and have held many official positions in our chapter. I worked to improve the curriculum of our temple's religious school.

Still, I missed the connection with the spirit of Judaism which I somehow had felt when growing up in my old neighborhood. I knew something was not quite answering my religious needs. I was relatively content with maintaining membership in our Reform temple. I did not attend services regularly, but wanted to attend more often—for social reasons rather than religious ones. I have many fond memories associated with those days, especially related to our chavura group, where we discussed topics of Jewish interest in each other's homes.

Not until my son embraced Orthodoxy and chose to be converted because of his Christian grandmother did I find the need to enhance my knowledge of Orthodox beliefs and observances. I started attending services at an Orthodox synagogue, and visited several other Orthodox synagogues with my husband and son.

Perhaps the seeds planted in my youth during my favorite class with our rabbi, discussing the Ethics of the Fathers, or my Youth Aliyah days with my friends, or just growing up in my Jewish neighborhood, or maybe—as someone once said of me—I have a Jewish soul; whatever it was, emotionally I felt as though I had come home. No longer feeling threatened by Orthodoxy, I consulted the Orthodox rabbi of the synagogue I was attending about conversion. He asked me enough questions to ascertain that I already had a strong Jewish identity, considerable knowledge of Jewish law and custom, and that I was serious about observance of the mitzvoth of Judaism. After a short process of study and review, I came before the Beth Din at the mikvah, with my daughter at my side. I underwent the conversion ceremony, something I had refused to do so many years ago.

At the mikvah, I expressed my enthusiastic affirmation of my desire to convert to Judaism and be accepted fully as a member of the Jewish people. After the immersion in the mikvah and the recitation of the blessings, I experienced a lovely feeling of accomplishment and satisfaction. I was congratulated by the rabbis and my daughter. It was a very positive, memorable experience. That night, our entire family enjoyed a special celebratory dinner in my honor.

The rabbi informed me that my husband and I now needed to be married according to Jewish law. I discussed this with my husband, and we both thought this would be a significant, pleasant, and memorable occasion. The wedding was arranged, and we soon found ourselves signing a document very much like the one we had signed many years earlier. The wedding was simple and beautiful, and the rabbis had even prepared a little reception with refreshments in honor of our wedding.

My husband has not chosen to adopt the Orthodox lifestyle. Yet he has been very accommodating to me, and very supportive of my religious interests. Shabbat and kashruth are special to me, and we do our best to maintain proper standards of observance. I am still learning, and continue to explore ways in which to more appropriately observe my new way of life.

When I attend the Orthodox synagogue, where men and women are seated in separate sections, I sometimes miss sitting next to my husband as we did at services in my former synagogue. But the positive attributes of Orthodox worship outweigh the difference in seating arrangements.

I hope that my experience will ease the way for others who may feel ready to convert, so that they may enhance their lives with the beautiful traditions and sanctity of Orthodox Jewish services and traditions.

*   *   *

The next essay was written by a young man who grew up in a Midwestern American city with a small Jewish population. From his early youth, he felt a strong affinity for Judaism, as though he had been born with a Jewish soul.

I'll never forget the moment I finally decided to convert. After promising myself year after year that my "next year in Jerusalem" would be as a Jew, I arrived at a crossroads. I was having my pre-Yom Kippur feast with my Jewish friend's family, as I had done for the past several years. I loved them, and they loved me. They were my Jewish "family." After we ate, "Mom" looked at me and said, "I never understand why you fast." I casually answered, "It's fun," to which she replied, "It's like making a mockery of Judaism." Ouch! To be sure, I didn't think it was fun to fast. I don't even know why I had responded in such a light manner, since in terms of Jewish practice I was more religious than she (maybe that was why I did not want to put on religious airs). At any rate, I was punched in the gut. I couldn't breathe as my eyes welled up. Immediately the rest of the family jumped in to defend me. But on some level, I knew she was right. What was I doing? So I didn't eat pork, so I kept Shabbat (mostly), so I lit Hanukkah candles: what did it all mean?

"Mom" came to apologize as I was getting dressed for the Kal Nidrei service. "I know you love Judaism," she said as she hugged me. I held in the tears, but as soon as I was alone again, the floodgates opened. What was I doing with my life, and what was God's plan for me?

I'd always believed in God, that He shaped my life and, indeed, brought me to Judaism. It was Truth, and I had found it! I had lived a nominally Jewish life for years, which astonished more people than I could understand. If I wasn't Jewish, why would I take Hebrew lessons, why would I fast on Yom Kippur, why would I so passionately defend Israel (as if you have to be Jewish to see the right and wrong there)? To me, it was the most natural thing in the world.

My family had no problem with my Jewish lifestyle. They found my Judaism charming. Gran would send me Rosh Hashana cards, Mom would wrap my Christmas presents in Hanukkah wrapping paper and buy dreidels, and she would pick up fresh challah for me every Friday. We'd even light Shabbat candles together. In fact, the most worrisome aspect of Judaism for Mom was letting the candles burn down by themselves. Dad called me his "little Jew." They were entirely supportive. Religion had been so peripheral to our lives that it was natural for them to associate Judaism in a like manner. We had Jewish friends, but how were they really different? I remember several years ago I wrote *mazal tov* in Hebrew on a graduation card to a daughter of my mom's friend, a Jewish friend, and she had no idea what it said. My mom was surprised. So that was their conception of Judaism—a nominal religiosity. Certainly no one trembled for my immortal soul.

Looking back to that fateful Yom Kippur, it was the most important day of my life. I had been jolted into reality by "Mom's" comment and then thrust into Kal Nidrei. My mind raced as the beauty and solemnity of that awesome service shook me to the core. Religiously, I believed Judaism was the truth. It was not even a question in my mind. To be sure, I had read and studied, and I knew that in Judaism it is not necessary for everyone in the world to become a Jew. I loved the Jewish people—I'd been to Israel twice, spoke Hebrew, and certainly identified culturally. Judaism demands action, however, and it was time for me to act on the courage of my convictions, or else resign myself to life as a gentile.

As we drove home that night (drove!), and sat on the couch to watch the television (as we did every year), I realized it just wasn't enough for me anymore. To identify with the Jewish people and celebrate their holidays was wonderful, but I needed to live a Judaism that wasn't merely Episcopalianism minus the trinity with a couple of bagels thrown in. I couldn't remain a "pseudo-Jew," as my brother referred to me, and yet live my authentic life. I am sure that I could have gone Reform or even Conservative to have a quick and easy conversion. It certainly would have been simpler. But in my heart I knew the truth. My soul belonged to the Jewish people, and I had to merge my destiny fully with theirs. It was time to step up and become part of the people of Israel on their terms, in the only acceptable way—halakhic conversion.

I remember the first time I saw the Kotel, the Western Wall in the Old City of Jerusalem. I had a sense of awe and transcendence, a feeling of homecoming. From that moment I knew my path. Such an instance of clarity occurred on that Yom Kippur. I finally had made up my mind.

I kept the conversion process very private. My friends and family noticed the increase in my observance level and lovingly teased me accordingly. Suddenly, everything had pork in it—"Don't drink that juice, it has bacon!" Or they would roll their eyes and complain that I wouldn't go out on Friday nights, dubbing me "super-Jew." Interestingly, it was mostly my Jewish friends who were perturbed, wondering why I was so fastidious when I "wasn't even really Jewish." They called Shabbat services "the cult," while my Christian friends called it "church." There were times I didn't think I would ever be fully Jewish, but ultimately my spiritual limbo was bearable as long as I kept studying and preparing for my future.

I had dreamed of how I would feel after the conversion, like I would emerge from the mikvah as a completely new person. To be sure, it was a profound experience, with gratitude and a sense of getting on with my life as a Jew the main emotions I felt. But it didn't fully hit me until the first Shabbat following my conversion, when I was called to the Torah. I had barely slept all night. I was nervous and excited, worried that I would somehow mess up and everyone would know I had been an outsider. I knew the procedure and I knew the blessings, and as I heard my name—my new Hebrew name—the realization set in. After months, indeed years, of being on the fringe, a pretend Jew watching from the outside, I was being called to the Torah as a Jew! It was thrilling. It still thrills me as I reflect on it today.

Being a Jew is such a privilege. At the risk of sounding slightly crazy, I believe that I have always had a Jewish soul and by some accident of birth was born to gentile parents. Now I have come back to Judaism, and I feel honored to be part of a glorious tradition that has brought such goodness and light to all of humankind, and to me personally. I didn't think I could possibly love Judaism or Israel more; but every day, as I put on my tefillin or recite the Shema, I feel my gratitude and wonder increase. I still get nervous when I am called to the Torah. Perhaps I always will. After all, it is quite an awesome experience. I only hope to prove myself worthy.

Chapter Seven

Motivations for Conversion

Although people tend to think about the conversion phenomenon in general terms, each individual convert has unique experiences, influences, spiritual struggles, and expectations. Each has been motivated to become Jewish by a unique set of reasons.

In the preceding chapter, we discussed Jewish ancestry as a motivation for conversion. In this chapter, we will focus on intellectual and spiritual considerations, marriage to a Jewish spouse, and the desire to be part of the Jewish people in Israel.

Seekers of Truth

Over the years, I have met with many prospective converts and have listened carefully to their stories. Among them has been a group that I call "seekers of truth." Highly spiritual and reflective, they are people who have searched for truth among different religions and philosophies, and have concluded that Judaism was most meaningful and true for them. Their spiritual quests were independent of considerations of marriage to a Jewish spouse or any other practical end. It was a matter of finding meaning and truth in life.

This group, as a whole, is characterized by intellectualism and spiritual sensitivity. Seekers of truth who convert to Judaism become serious Jews, religiously active and involved. In many cases, they are fully integrated into their congregations and have married Jewish spouses and raised Jewish children. To a certain extent, people of this kind are ideal converts, because they come to Judaism purely from intellectual and spiritual considerations.

Several of the seekers of truth with whom I am acquainted actually were raised in an environment that fostered anti-Semitism. One was a member of a white-supremacist group before it dawned upon him that hatred of Jews, blacks, and other minorities was self-destructive behavior that deprived him of genuine happiness. He began to study Judaism as a way of overcoming his previous hatred; and then came to love Judaism and yearned to become part of the Jewish people. He not only converted, but went on to be a leader and teacher in the small Jewish community in which he lived.

Another was the daughter of a university president who was known to harbor anti-Semitic views. She grew up with anti-Jewish prejudices, in a liberal Protestant denomination, and was as surprised as her father that she ultimately found truth and meaning in Judaism. Her turn to Judaism was the result of a long process of study, trial and error, and interaction with Jews who belied the anti-Semitic stereotypes with which she had been raised.

Yet another grew up in an Arab country notoriously hostile to Jews. She eventually moved to the United States, where she came to realize the viciousness and falseness of the images of Jews presented to her by the propaganda of her birth country. She pursued her quest for truth, and concluded that she wanted to join the Jewish people. After her conversion, she made the following observation: "In my idealistic way, I sometimes wish I could wave a magic wand and make everyone who hated anyone *become* that person, race, or religion, just to see how ugly and poisonous hatred is, and how it robs the haters of life. The choice to convert is a conscious decision not to hate but to love, and to embrace others—not just Jews—to show that God is the God of all the world, not just Jewry."

A doctoral student of comparative religion, who converted to Judaism after many years of study and thought, described her acceptance of Judaism:

I was not "shopping" for a new religion. In retrospect, I wasn't shopping for a particular form of Judaism. I was asking myself what it would mean for me to live a Jewish life. The answers came from a number of different sources over the years—people, books, and individual reflection. Meanwhile, I began to live some of the rhythms of a Jewish life. . . . My decision to convert to Judaism thus flowed naturally from the life I had begun to live and wished to validate formally. It marked not an end to questions about family, faith and religion, but rather the beginning of continued exploration of such questions within the context of Judaism. And by Judaism, I refer not only to the particular traditions of family and synagogue, but also to the timeless and time-bound traditions of Jewish communities throughout history. It is therefore difficult for me to articulate "why Orthodox Judaism" when I hold dear both the particular and universal expressions of a Jewish life.

An M.I.T.-trained Ph.D., raised in a southern state, converted to Judaism at age forty-eight. As a youngster, he was raised in a religious Christian family, but he dropped out of the church by age fifteen. He found himself unable to believe in a number of the church's teachings, and decided to search for truth on his own. In college, he studied philosophy and science. He could believe in the God of creation, but did not believe in a God to whom one could pray. It took many years before he developed a sense of God's immanence as well as His transcendence. How this happened he himself cannot fully explain. It was, in effect, a leap of faith that grew out of his years of contemplation and experience.

Not all of the seekers of truth ultimately succeed in converting to Judaism. Some stop along the way because they do not feel able to accept the total commitment that conversion entails. Some seem unable to make any fateful decision, but spend their years vacillating within a spiritual limbo.

It must be stated candidly that not all seekers of truth are psychologically healthy. I have met individuals who indeed were intel-

lectually and spiritually searching for truth, but who were also emotionally troubled. They hoped they would find solace in Judaism
and the Jewish community, and that they would somehow solve
their deep-seated problems by converting. Conversion, though,
does not magically cure emotional problems.

I have also known converts who have embraced Judaism after a
long process of spiritual struggle, and who became quite observant
religious Jews. After a number of years, however, they again
became spiritually restless and actually left their Jewish spouses
and children to try out another religious path. In the few instances
of which I am personally aware, these seekers of truth did not return
to their birth religions, but were attracted to Eastern religions. It is
possible that they will one day leave those Eastern religions in
search of yet another spiritual path—possibly even returning to
Judaism.

Conversion for the Sake of Marriage

The Talmud tells a dramatic story about a young Torah scholar
who was drawn to a harlot.[51] Before he could sin with her, though,
he remembered the tsitsith (four-cornered ritual garment with
fringes) that he was wearing; and he refrained from sin. He went
back to the academy of Rabbi Hiyya, where he was a student.

The harlot was quite impressed by the young man whose religious convictions had overcome his physical urges. She went to
Rabbi Hiyya and requested that he convert her to Judaism. He
asked her: "My daughter, perhaps you have fallen in love with one
of the students here?" She answered yes. She told him what had
happened, and how impressed she was with the young man. Rabbi
Hiyya approved her as a candidate for conversion, and presumably
she eventually married the student.

Although the impetus for the harlot's conversion was her admi-
ration for a man and her desire to marry him, this did not disquali-

---

[51] Menahot 44a

fy her as a prospective proselyte. Rabbi Hiyya obviously sensed that she was attracted not just to the man, but to his virtue; she wanted to become part of a virtuous, righteous society. Rashi, commenting on the Talmudic story, notes that the harlot assured Rabbi Hiyya that her desire to convert was "for the sake of Heaven." Certainly, Rabbi Hiyya thought that she would ultimately convert based on her commitment to Torah—not on her love of a man.

In fact, many converts have been brought to Judaism by an initial desire to marry a Jew. Halakha looks askance at conversions of convenience, even if it does not disqualify such conversions outright. It is up to rabbis to determine the sincerity of the would-be converts and to instruct them so that they convert "for the sake of Heaven"—from conviction, not convenience.

A candidate for conversion needs to understand that the conversion must not be contingent on a relationship with a Jewish partner. It must be an independent decision based on the candidate's awareness that conversion is not revocable—that a convert's Jewishness will continue even if the relationship with the Jewish partner should end, and therefore that conversion is a profound matter for which one is ultimately answerable to God.

Over twenty years ago, I was involved in an unusual case of conversion for the sake of marriage. A young woman, raised in a thoroughly Orthodox family, fell in love with a non-Jewish man. The woman had attended all-female Orthodox schools from nursery through college. She was completely observant, and dedicated to Jewish religion and the Jewish people. There was no doubt in her mind that she wanted to raise Orthodox Jewish children. Yet, even with her background and high level of religious knowledge and commitment, she wanted to marry a non-Jewish man. He was a fine, upstanding person, intelligent, professionally successful, and he very much wanted to marry her. He was willing to have his children raised as Orthodox Jews. However, he himself was not particularly drawn to Judaism, and did not especially want to convert.

The woman was ready to marry him even if he did not convert

to Judaism. Her parents, though, were adamant that she should not marry out of the faith. They wanted the couple to speak with an Orthodox rabbi to see what could be done; and, through family members, the couple found their way to me.

Our first meeting was cordial and candid. The man seemed ambivalent about conversion, although he expressed willingness to go through the process to keep peace in the family. I explained that conversion was a serious matter that required a strong personal commitment to Judaism, and that it shouldn't be undertaken merely for the sake of marriage. After some subsequent discussions, he agreed to prepare himself for conversion. I wasn't absolutely convinced of his sincerity at the time, but I felt that we should at least try to see the process through.

The period of study was valuable to him. He began to intensify his religious observance and involvement. He quickly mastered the basic texts, he learned Hebrew, he grew more comfortable with synagogue and home rituals. To all appearances, he had reached the point where he would qualify as an excellent convert; and yet I still wondered about his interior life. Yes, he was saying and doing all the right things; but did he really believe in them? I reached the point where I felt confident enough that his commitment was genuine. The conversion took place, the couple married, and shortly thereafter they moved to a city on the West Coast. They kept in touch with me for a while, and let me know that they had become active members of the Orthodox congregation in their town. Then I did not hear from them for over ten years.

When one of their sons was ready to celebrate his Bar Mitzvah, they decided to have a dinner in honor of the occasion in the New York area so that the New York relatives could more easily attend. Thoughtfully, they invited my wife and me to this dinner. We accepted. We attended. We were pleased beyond words.

The Bar Mitzvah boy and his siblings were obviously being brought up in the Orthodox Jewish tradition. They were students in a Jewish day school, and were very comfortable discussing words of Torah. Seeing the family together, no outside observer could have guessed that the children's father had started as a somewhat unenthusiastic candidate for conversion to Judaism. He was so naturally involved in everything; he was obviously a very good, religious Jewish husband and father. When he spoke, we were particularly moved. He expressed his pride in his Bar Mitzvah son's accomplishments as a *ben Torah*, a young man devoted to the Torah way of life. Indeed, his speech was so thoroughly imbued with love of Torah that one would have thought that he had been Orthodox all his life. I have rarely heard such eloquent, heartfelt, and meaningful words from a father to his son at a Bar Mitzvah occasion.

What had begun as a somewhat cool agreement to convert for the sake of marriage had obviously developed into an all-encompassing commitment to Torah. This is a classic example of how a conversion process that starts for the sake of marriage can develop into a conversion for its own sake. What a great loss it would have been for the convert, his family, and the Jewish people if he had been turned away from Judaism rather than encouraged to convert.

*   *   *

The following essays were written by women whose decision to convert to Judaism was prompted by their desire to marry Jews. It will be noted that each of them came to accept Judaism on its own terms, and that the conversions, in the final analysis, were for the sake of Heaven. The first essay is by a woman who grew up in the South and had little direct contact with Jews or Judaism.

My family of origin were Methodists and serious about it. Every Sunday morning we attended Sunday school and church services together. Every Sunday evening, the young people attended MYF (Methodist Youth Fellowship) and the entire family attended evening worship. Every Wednesday was evening prayer meeting. This was not unusual in the small-town Deep South of the 1950s.

My extended family, my friends, my teachers, most people I knew attended church regularly. It is not something anyone ever thought to question. We grew up learning and reading the Bible (Old and New Testaments) without realizing there might be alternatives.

My small town (one traffic light) had one Jewish resident. He was well-liked and known to everyone as "Happy" Loeb. His wife was a Methodist, and in the same Sunday school class with my mother. (Sunday school is for all ages, not just children.) I didn't meet another Jew until I attended Millsaps College. Students who went to Millsaps thought of it as an oasis in the Deep South. The widespread belief was that Millsaps' entering freshman classes were consistently in the top 1 percent academically of the nation's entering freshman classes, although I'm not sure anyone ever actually verified this. This small Methodist college attracted a wide variety of students of diverse religious backgrounds who took every opportunity to question and explore. It was everything a college should be. One of the things we explored was religion. I learned a little about Judaism and went with a Jewish friend from Millsaps to services at the Reform temple in town.

Several years later, I was a teacher at a junior high school in Maryland, when I met S. As teachers in the same small school with a fairly close faculty, we naturally were acquainted with each other. We spent time together and gradually realized how similar our values are. (Neither of us had any interest in marriage at the time.) As we became better acquainted, S. told me much of what he knew about Judaism. I had many questions, and S. did not always know the answer. We began to learn together. We began attending a Reform temple, since it presented the least Hebrew barrier. We became regulars at every Friday night service. (It was a constant source of amusement to us when we had attended every week for two or three years that members who attended only occasionally would welcome us as newcomers because they had not seen us before.)

Having always questioned things, I had been fortunate that

Methodists are much more tolerant of questions than many religions. Imagine my delight to learn that Judaism not only tolerates but actually encourages questioning.

Although S. and I had not considered marriage, we began to realize how well suited we are to each other. I had become comfortable with Judaism and the compassion for others it teaches in so many ways. We both wanted to learn more about Judaism, and I began to consider conversion.

I went to an Orthodox rabbi and asked how I might learn more about Judaism and ultimately convert. He asked if I wanted to convert in order to marry a Jew. I answered no. Although S. and I were indeed considering marriage, I wanted to convert to become Jewish, not to be married. The rabbi told me quite firmly to go away and be a good gentile. I left.

We then asked the rabbi of the Reform temple we attended how to proceed. He was encouraging. He had left retirement to lead the congregation; because of his age he no longer worked with conversion candidates. He referred us to a Reform rabbi in a nearby city. We met with the rabbi and joined a conversion class for couples newly married or soon to be married. I felt that this definition was too restrictive. I was not attending the introduction to Judaism class simply because I was planning to marry a Jew. I was attending the class because I wanted to learn more about Judaism. Over a four-month period, S. and I attended the series of classes and read the six or seven books required. We discussed them; we both grew in our knowledge and understanding of Judaism. At the conclusion of the classes, we went back to our rabbi, who performed the Reform conversion ceremony for me.

During the three years S. and I had been dating, I had not met his parents. My family welcomed S. His friends and his brother accepted me. But I was not welcome in his parents' home. Once the Reform conversion had taken place, though, S.'s parents accepted me and welcomed me without reservation.

As I became better acquainted with Jews and Judaism, I began to understand some of the differences within Judaism. We still attended the Reform services because neither of us knew more than a few words of Hebrew. I still wanted an Orthodox conversion. I wanted to be sure that if we had children, there would be no question as to their Jewishness. Fortunately, S.'s father was a close friend of an Orthodox rabbi, and this rabbi was willing to help. Since I lived in Maryland and the rabbi was in New York, he arranged for a rabbinical friend of his in our area to study with me. S. and I read the entire Torah with commentary, and discussed our readings regularly. I learned the rules of kashruth and began to keep kasher. When the rabbi in our area thought I was ready, the New York rabbi arranged for my Orthodox conversion.

Since becoming Jewish, I have continued to study and read. I have worked particularly hard at learning Hebrew. Although it took me three years to make the *kh* sound, I finally mastered it. I can read Hebrew and write cursive. I know some modern conversational Hebrew.

S. and I have continued growing in our Jewish knowledge and observance. We are fortunate to live in an area where, although the Jewish community is small, Judaism is alive and well and active. S. is involved in synagogue life, and recently served as president of the congregation. At the university where I teach, I helped organize the first Hillel, and have served as the faculty adviser for many years. The rabbi of our congregation is always helpful and encourages congregants to grow in their religious observance. He has incorporated some of our own family customs into the general pattern of the synagogue tradition.

S. and I have one son, now twenty-three. He attended the local Hebrew day school through fifth grade, and received an excellent foundation in Judaism. His involvement continued with Sunday school, Hebrew high school, Jewish youth groups and summer camps, and summer study in Israel at Alexander Muss High School. When he began considering which university to attend, his one non-negotiable criterion was a sizeable Jewish population.

My family of origin and I have always had a good relationship and continue to do so. However, as I explained my decision to convert to Judaism to my mother and my sisters, they had different reactions. (My father had died several years earlier.) I especially tried to emphasize that we all believe in the same God, and stressed our similarities rather than our differences. Still, choice of religion is a subject we generally avoid. About ten years after my conversion to Judaism, my mother had not mentioned my conversion, and I interpreted her silence as acceptance. I told her that I understood that it was difficult for her, and that I appreciated her accepting my decision to become Jewish. Her reply was simply, "I haven't accepted it." Since then we have not brought up the topic again. This is a source of sadness for me, that my conversion brought unhappiness to my mother. She loves me and my husband and son. She attended our son's Bar Mitzvah. She sees that I have a good marriage and a loving family. We live 700 miles apart, but visit regularly and speak almost daily. I regret that my mother is unhappy, but she feels sure that I will spend eternity in hell.

Although we are close and all love each other and support each other, only one sister has accepted my decision to convert. Another sister still has reservations. Recently she asked me if I would give up Judaism if something happened to my husband. She was quite surprised when I told her that I would continue to be Jewish. I suppose she thinks I became Jewish only for my husband's sake. I became Jewish because it feels right. I am a part of the Jewish people. I identify with the concepts and beliefs, the levels of charity, the philosophy that only the injured party can forgive, that people should live ethical lives because it is the right thing to do, not for promise of reward or threat of punishment. These things make much sense to me. I am continually finding areas of Judaism where I can only marvel at how logical and intelligent the solutions are. I can question and reason and decide for myself. Even the word

"Israel" can be interpreted as "struggle with God." With Judaism, I feel I have found where I was destined to be all along. I am a part of the larger whole.

*   *   *

The next essay reflects some of the complexities in a conversion for the sake of marriage.

I was raised a Catholic but spent most of my childhood with a Jewish stepfather. We celebrated holidays of the Jewish and Catholic faiths, but rarely attended services. I met my husband when I was twenty years old, and we married less than two months later. On the way to elope, my soon-to-be husband asked me to make him one promise: that I convert to Judaism immediately! It was an easy promise to make for love. More important, and in retrospect, I realize that I was looking for some new meaning in my life. I had been raised in a broken home, and I believe that I had always missed the feeling of complete family unity. The new lifestyle and customs that I was sharing with my husband created a happy environment for me. As a couple then, and even now after twenty years, our interest in Judaism has given us something in common.

Keeping my promise to convert entailed more obstacles than I could have imagined. Within a year, I had become a mother; life was busy. Conversion was a priority matter for both my husband and me. We were initially discouraged by the response we received as to how long it might take to complete an Orthodox conversion. Hence, we decided to take the Reform route. It was not long before my husband figured out that this was not the right fit for him. By the end of the first course in Reform Judaism, we were on our way to England— my husband's birthplace and site of a new business. We went to the Beth Din there, and I could see almost immediately that my quest to attain an Orthodox conversion would be tough work.

I spent the next two years adhering to what I considered to be a very strict religious lifestyle. We were strictly kosher, only eating out at kosher restaurants and homes. We walked miles to synagogue each Shabbat—usually in the rain. Every six months, I made an appearance before the Beth Din only to have my request for a prompt conversion denied. Others told me that this was part of the process, to see how committed I was; and this actually made sense to me. But it did become discouraging, particularly since I was so far from family and friends in America. Fortunately, my husband decided on a move back to the United States. What lay ahead of me in my work to convert would be encouraging, inspiring, educational, and deeply spiritual.

I now had two children and was back in New York. D. and I had been married four years, and my in-laws were very supportive of my conversion, which initially was a painful subject for them. My parents had never been averse to my converting, but wondered if I was giving too much of myself to the process. Over time, they have come to see my life and the lives of their grandchildren infinitely enriched by Judaism.

My husband's parents arranged for me to meet their rabbi, an Orthodox rabbi, shortly after our return to New York. I distinctly remember the meeting. I was nervous about what to wear and what to say, but I was immediately put at ease by the rabbi's words of encouragement and understanding. I explained to him the extent of my study and observance; he felt that I was close to where I needed to be in order to convert. What followed was an intense period of reading and learning. Over the next year, I managed to do a great amount of reading while still caring for my husband and children. Although my road to conversion was long, I believe it gave more meaning to what would be the foundation of my role as wife, mother, and plainly speaking, the person I wanted to be.

Going to the mikvah, and having our children duly converted as well, was a magical moment for me. Following my conversion, my husband and I were married again according to Jewish law—six years after our original wedding!

What a sense of accomplishment and relief I felt in the months after I completed my conversion. Soon, though, we were on our way to make a life in the Midwestern town where my mother lived. The move turned out to be a wonderful decision for a variety of reasons, but it posed difficult questions as to how we could live a religious Jewish life. In 1991, the town to which we moved had no synagogue, no Hebrew school, and certainly no kasher butcher.

The move became an adventure for my husband and me. It brought us close together and even closer to our (now three) children. They were young when we arrived in Wyoming, and it soon became evident that they would need Jewish instruction. They would sometimes be the only Jewish children in their classes in public school. They tell me now that they came to feel an even greater connection to their own Judaism because of the efforts we all have made to remember who we are. My husband helped me start the first Sunday Hebrew school in town, with a dozen children attending. Our son, through local instruction and under the constant supervision of our rabbi in New York, was the first Bar Mitzvah in our area, and then had another ceremony in honor of his Bar Mitzvah at our synagogue in New York.

Our town now boasts a Jewish community of about 300. I no longer need to bake my own challah or fly in kosher meat from Denver; these things are available in our community. We have a wonderful rabbi who has been particularly kind and receptive to converts, and this has been a source of satisfaction to me as I remember my own conversion and how much my life had changed for the better because of it. We are happy that our family plays an active role in the life of our Jewish community.

*   *   *

The next essay is a candid reflection on conversion for the sake of marriage, where the convert has accepted a basically Orthodox lifestyle, but has not altogether transformed her pre-conversion feelings about life.

My introduction to Judaism, eventual Orthodox conversion, and almost total immersion in the religion came as a surprise to me, and is honestly not something that I would have sought out or chosen for myself under ordinary circumstances. I was brought up as a Christian Scientist, a non-mainstream Christian denomination. The teachings are based on both the Old and New Testaments of the Bible, and offer a metaphysical approach to thinking and healing as the basis of the religion. At the time I was growing up, it seemed to be controversial to rely on the power of the mind and trust in God for physical healing, although today, the mind/body connection is much more widely accepted.

The fact that I happened to fall in love with someone Jewish is what ultimately set off the chain of events leading to my conversion to Judaism. During our courtship, my husband said that he would like our children to be raised as Jews, and I did not have a problem with that. I realized that he was uncomfortable, to say the least, with my religion. Since I felt that religious foundation was very important, I agreed to Judaism. What I did not realize at the time was that as a "condition" of our marriage I would need to convert so that our children would be born Jewish. I never would have imagined this to be the case. Wasn't love enough? My knowledge prior to this time of anything to do with Judaism was virtually nil. It did not occur to me that there could be a requirement for me to convert in order to have Jewish children. It seemed logical to me that we, as parents, could simply choose a religion in which to bring our children up, and that would be that.

As I began the conversion process, I looked at the conversion as though I were merely adding Jewish customs and ideals to the foundation and love of God that I already had, not that I was changing myself or my spirituality in any way. I was just adding to them. This thought made it somewhat easier for me to deal with the conversion. My husband grew up on a kibbutz in Israel and was not particularly religious when I met him. I assumed that our lifestyle would be something along the lines of Reform Judaism. But it turned out that I was wrong. Beginning with the conversion, the whole thing began to snowball; I soon realized that a basic conversion was not sufficient—it had to be an Orthodox conversion. This was the only way to have acceptance in the State of Israel, where most of my husband's family reside.

At this point, I was so committed to the relationship that I agreed. The conversion process was actually quite engaging. It involved dedicated and intense study with a rabbi, and offered interesting insights to the familiar Biblical stories I already knew from my own experience. It was truly an addition to the knowledge and understanding of the Bible that I already had, which was what I anticipated, plus an additional set of customs and holidays. At that point, I still felt that I was not actually changing or letting go of any of my past—just embellishing it to include Jewish practices.

Nevertheless, I was able to complete my conversion studies and was converted under the auspices of an Orthodox Beth Din. My husband and I then got married. We did not live a particularly Orthodox lifestyle, though, and when it was time for our eldest daughter to go to preschool, we enrolled her in a Reform Jewish day school in our neighborhood. It turned out, though, that our daughter was not happy at school. To this day, we are not sure whether she was simply uncomfortable in the school environment, or whether it was a developmental issue or her young age. After two years in this situation, where things did not seem to be improving, we moved her to an Orthodox school that had an excellent reputation for its early childhood program, and came highly recommended by an acquaintance of my husband. This transition was really the beginning of our entry into the Orthodox world. Until this point, we really were just on the fringes looking in. Our daughter responded well to the nurturing environment of the new school and flourished there. Eventually, her two siblings were also enrolled in this school.

Being part of the school community, it was necessary that we uphold the basic tenets of Judaism to the best of our ability. This included maintaining a kasher household so that our children's friends would be comfortable in our home. All of our children have since transferred to another yeshiva, and we are all the more immersed in the fabric of both our synagogue and school communities, and have adapted as best we can to the modern Orthodox lifestyle which characterizes our social network.

It is many years later, and personally I have to admit that inwardly I still do not consider myself to have been entirely transformed into a Jewish identity, although I am happy to uphold the ideals. For me, the striving to become a better and more loving person is what is ultimately important, and not the label of a particular religious faith.

Love of Israel

Rabbi Haim David Halevy identified three major categories of converts to Judaism. The first includes those who come to Judaism as a result of study and spiritual attraction, those whom I call seekers of truth. The second is composed of those who convert for the sake of marriage. The third are those who wish to convert because of their desire to be part of the modern State of Israel.[52] Israel is a young, idealistic country; it strives to create a just, democratic society even while constantly under attack by its hate-filled enemies. Israel is a beacon of hope for those seeking a meaningful life in a vibrant society. Especially to young men and women growing up in materialistic or spiritually sterile environments, Israel offers a

---

[52] Rabbi Haim David Halevy, *Asei Lekha Rav* 3:29

tremendously attractive alternative.

Some non-Jewish young people have settled in Israel not from a religious motivation to live a life of Torah and mitzvoth, but from a desire to become part of the drama of a growing new country or to escape from persecution and instability in the lands of their birth. Those who ultimately are willing to accept the mitzvoth can be converted, just like those who originally were drawn to Judaism for the sake of marriage. However, what about those who live among non-religious Israeli Jews and have no particular interest in making religious commitments?

Rabbi Halevy states that rabbinical courts should not accept for conversion anyone who clearly articulates an antipathy to Torah and mitzvoth. In the final analysis, though, it is up to the rabbinical court to decide how to deal with candidates for conversion whose prime motivation is nationalistic rather than religious. This is not merely a matter that affects the conversion of individuals, but also has national importance for the social fabric of the State of Israel. Is it a good idea to turn away from conversion a person who has decided to live in Israel and become part of Israeli society? Won't such individuals gradually integrate themselves into Israeli life, and wouldn't it be better if they do so as bona fide Jews with halakhic conversions? Each case, of course, needs to be considered on its own merits. If it is decided to accept such individuals as candidates for conversion, then the rabbis should see to it that they are given proper religious instruction, and perhaps even have them live for a while in religious settlements where they can experience religious life more fully.

Rabbi Halevy considers the opinions of some rabbis who oppose taking in converts whose level of religious observance is deficient. They cite the Talmudic dictum that we do not accept for conversion a person who rejects even one detail of the mitzvoth. Rabbi Halevy explains that these rabbis cite this passage erroneously. What it means is that we do not accept a candidate for conversion if he has studied the Torah and then says that he does not accept a certain detail.

> But one who has not studied or researched or understood, and he
> rejects a certain detail or even the entire Oral Torah—this person
> is not yet considered a denier, as we have explained in the case
> confronting Hillel. [Hillel accepted a candidate for conversion
> who rejected the Oral Torah.][53] It is permissible to accept him if
> one can hope that after the person studies, he will indeed accept
> [even this detail that he currently rejects].

Since the Talmud only requires that we inform would-be candidates of some of the mitzvoth, it is obvious that the person is not in
a position to accept them all in every detail. So how can we ever
accept converts? "If he accepted the whole Torah and all the
mitzvoth in a general way, even without knowing [their full content,
and was converted on this basis], and when he subsequently learns
yet does not fulfill them . . . he is still a complete convert and is like
a sinning Jew."

Rabbi Halevy's approach is to be as open and receptive to such
converts as possible, because converting them is generally a better
alternative for them and for Israeli society as a whole. As long as
they give general assent to Torah and mitzvoth, even if they do not
know all the details—and even if in their hearts they have no real
commitment to keep the mitzvoth—these individuals are still valid
converts according to halakha.

Rabbi Yehuda Issar Unterman, late Ashkenazic Chief Rabbi of
Israel, did not approve of conversions for the sake of marriage
when he lived in England. He felt that such converts would basically continue to lead their accustomed lifestyle and would not
really experience a religious transformation. However, he did
approve of such conversions in Israel. Since the converts—even if
they came to Judaism for ulterior motives, such as marriage and

---

[53] Shabbat 31a.

love of Israel—were living in a thoroughly Jewish society, they would indeed have a transformation of identity and would become fully Jewish in outlook.[54]

With the arrival in Israel of many thousands of non-Jewish spouses of Russian Jews, the issue of conversion has gained in urgency. Many, if not most, of these non-Jewish spouses have not come to Israel for primarily religious reasons. Their motivation for conversion is more for personal/national considerations than for love of Torah and mitzvoth. Yet it is vital for Israeli society to integrate these people into the fabric of Jewish life and identity; halakhic conversion is the way this can be done. Fortunately, a number of rabbis in Israel have taken the responsibility to teach these individuals and lead them to conversion. Are all of these candidates for conversion going to become fully observant of Torah and mitzvoth? No. Nevertheless, using the logic of such sages as Rabbi Halevy and Rabbi Unterman, many can achieve halakhic conversion. By living in Israel, they are certainly demonstrating a commitment to a Jewish way of life.[55]

---

[54] *Noam*, no. 14, Jerusalem, 5731, pp. 1–9.

[55] See Moshe Samet's article, "Gerut ve-Tsionut," in *Sefer ha-Yovel le-Rav Mordecai Breuer*, pp. 487–508. Samet cites the responsa of some nineteenth- and twentieth-century halakhic authorities who were lenient in matters of conversion. He points out that sages who espoused Zionism were more receptive to conversion than those who were anti-Zionist.

Chapter Eight

Practical Considerations

Conversion to Judaism is a significant and growing phenomenon. Decisions about conversion today will have a continuing impact for generations to come.

The argument of this book is that the Orthodox community needs to be actively engaged in helping would-be converts to enter the fold of Israel. Since non-halakhic conversions are so problematic for the future of the Jewish people, it is vital that realistic halakhic alternatives be encouraged. The halakha provides a meaningful and accessible way for non-Jews to join the Jewish people and religion.

This book includes essays by halakhic converts that let us understand the issue of conversion from the perspective of those who have actually undergone the process. The Jewish people is better and stronger for having such individuals as part of our community. They have joined us of their own free will, conscious of the risks and responsibilities inherent in being Jewish. They have become active participants in their synagogues and communities, and often have risen to positions of leadership.

It must be stressed, though, that not everyone who wishes to convert can actually be accepted by Orthodox rabbis. Yes, Rabbi Uziel and other halakhic authorities have called on rabbis to expedite conversions to prevent intermarriage and to keep children within the Jewish fold. But there are cases that even the most lenient halakhists cannot undertake; namely, where the would-be convert specifically rejects basic Jewish beliefs and observances, and expresses an unwillingness to accept them. There are other cases where a rabbi may have doubts about whether to accept a convert. This includes situations where the candidate for conversion seems to lack sincerity because the conversion is merely for convenience, not principle. The operative Talmudic principle holds that "the judge only has what his eyes see." Each rabbi ultimately must pass judgment based on his own understanding and sensitivity.

Various factors go into the decision to accept a proselyte. Sometimes, even when the candidate for conversion says all the right things, a rabbi's intuition tells him that the applicant should be rejected. The rabbi may sense that the would-be convert has severe emotional problems and is looking to Judaism as an escape from life's troubles. Such candidates need to work out their problems with psychological counseling before being accepted for conversion.

Other candidates for conversion are not really interested in Judaism or Jewish identity—they simply want to marry a Jewish person. The Jewish partner has dragged the non-Jewish one to the rabbi, often at the insistence of parents. The couple plans to be married regardless of what the rabbi says. They go through the motions of inquiring about conversion but do not take conversion seriously as a life-transforming process. What they really want from the rabbi is a quick, easy way to assuage guilt feelings or parental pressures; they want the rabbi to clean up their dilemma by giving halakhic sanction to their relationship. Understandably, rabbis are not keen to undertake responsibility for conversions under such circumstances.

Rabbis who are called upon to guide would-be converts must take their responsibility very seriously. They must ascertain that the candidate for conversion is sincere, willing to identify fully with the Jewish people, and willing to study and observe mitzvoth. Conversion entails a process of study and reflection, and should not be performed perfunctorily or quickly. Nor should a candidate for conversion expect the rabbi to give an exact timetable for the conversion. Candidates absorb Judaism and Jewishness at their own individual pace; the process should not be truncated.

While rabbis can point with pride to converts who have become righteous proselytes, they unfortunately can also point to converts who have disappointed them. Some would-be converts seem enthusiastic enough at the beginning of the process, and even through the conversion itself. Thereafter, though, their level of interest and observance may drop off.

Others may continue with a high level of interest and observance, but may manifest emotional or social problems. When rabbis have been disappointed in their converts, they may well tend to shy away from taking responsibility for future candidates for conversion.

General Guidelines for Conversion

As a general rule, would-be converts should study under the guidance of an Orthodox rabbi, and should live in the neighborhood of the rabbi's synagogue. Although much of the actual studying can be done with a tutor, it is essential for the candidate to have ready access to the rabbi. A good rabbi/student relationship helps both parties build the confidence to reach the goal of conversion. If the candidate attends the rabbi's synagogue and becomes part of his community, the rabbi can assist the candidate in adjusting to the communal context. The rabbi can introduce the candidate to congregants who can provide friendship, hospitality, and kindness.

When a would-be convert has a Jewish partner or spouse, it is advisable that the Jewish person study the same texts as the candidate for conversion. This is an opportunity for both of them to grow in their Jewishness and to learn Torah together. Unless the Jewish partner is actively engaged in study and observance, conflicts may arise as the would-be convert starts taking Judaism more seriously. I know of cases where the non-Jewish candidate for conversion became so committed to Torah and mitzvah observance that the Jewish partner, who was not as religiously inclined, felt uncomfortable. In some instances, couples have actually broken up over religious issues.

To deepen one's sense of community, the would-be convert should participate in Jewish communal life (religious, charitable, social, educational) and identify with the Jewish people everywhere, including the State of Israel. A visit to Israel or an extended stay there can be a valuable, life-changing experience.

A candidate for conversion must study the Torah and become familiar with Jewish beliefs and the requirements of Jewish law. The candidate must not only understand the religion intellectually, but must learn to observe the commandments so that they become a natural part of life. This is a process that takes considerable time and effort. The would-be convert should study the Torah with an appropriate traditional Jewish commentary, should learn at least enough Hebrew to be fluent in reading the prayers and reciting the blessings, and should be familiar with the structure and content of the Siddur (prayer book), and with the basic laws and customs of Judaism. It is desirable that the student attend classes in an Orthodox synagogue and read extensively to gain as much knowledge as possible about Jewish traditions, history, and philosophy.

The candidate for conversion must accept the responsibilities of being Jewish with free will and with awareness of the consequences of this decision. Even if the conversion process began in order to please a Jewish friend, the ultimate decision must be made solely and completely by the person who wishes to convert. Candidates for conversion must be certain that they are making the right decision, because conversion to Judaism is permanent and not revocable. Since this is such a serious decision, the would-be convert must be comfortable and happy with the decision to accept Judaism and a Jewish identity.

The process of conversion is challenging and demanding. It involves much thinking, reshaping of attitudes, reorganizing patterns of living. A person who wishes to convert according to halakha should find the process meaningful and challenging. The Jewish people welcomes individuals who have fulfilled the halakhic requirements for conversion and who sincerely and freely join the people of Israel.

The actual arrangement of the circumcision and ritual immersion should be supervised by a competent rabbinic court under the direction of an Orthodox rabbi. The convert will choose a Hebrew name, often taken from the Bible, by which he or she will be known for Jewish religious purposes.

Obviously, the period of preparation for conversion will vary from person to person. The process must be accepted as an open-ended spiritual adventure. When the appropriate time arrives for the actual conversion ceremony, both the would-be convert and the rabbi will know.

Converts as Models of Inspiration

Some years ago I received a letter from a thirty-two-year-old man, studying for conversion to Judaism, who lives in the Midwest. He wrote:

> I am descended from many members of Shearith Israel. While both my father's parents were Jewish, he was not raised in a religious home. My mother is not Jewish and I was not raised Jewish at all. I have been doing my family genealogy for several years now, and have come to the conclusion that I have lost something great by not having been raised Jewish. The more I learn about Judaism, and especially the long line of Jews that came before me, I think it would be the ultimate in arrogance for me to ignore my place in that line.

How poignant that this man, separated from Jewish life from birth, was trying to find his way back to his ancestral faith and people. In my subsequent discussions with him, I was impressed with his sincerity and enthusiasm.

Sometimes, a person looking at Judaism from the outside can help born Jews to appreciate its beauty and depth. We do not always take stock of what we have, nor do we always recognize how important it is for us to live according to the teachings of Judaism. To convey the Jewish way of life to our children and grandchildren, we ourselves need to feel the special excitement and privilege of being Jewish.

Ordained to Be a Jew is a fascinating book by John David Scalamonti, a former Catholic priest who is now an Orthodox Jew. The book tells the remarkable story of his decision to become a member of the Jewish people, to observe the laws and traditions of the Torah. He points out that many non-Jews, through no fault of their own, know very little about Judaism. "There are Jews, too, who do not know the essence of their faith. What little I know of Judaism, what little I have experienced in Judaism, is enough for me to regret that I was not born a Jew, and enough for me to attempt to persuade those born in the faith to appreciate their religious heritage and live it to the fullest."[56]

I have learned much from converts over the course of my years in the rabbinate. I have been inspired by their devotion, their fresh and honest approach to Jewish tradition. I have been challenged by their questions, impressed by their intellectual struggles and their spiritual courage. Converts are a valuable resource for the Jewish people, not only increasing our numbers but increasing our appreciation of the eternal and universal teachings of Judaism.

The Book of Ruth records that Boaz was deeply moved by

---

[56] *Ordained to Be a Jew: A Catholic Priest's Conversion to Judaism*, Ktav Publishing House, Hoboken, N.J., 1992, p. 172.

Ruth's faithfulness to her mother-in-law Naomi, "and how you have left your father and your mother and the land of your birth, and have come [to join] a people you did not know heretofore." Boaz blesses Ruth with a blessing that is appropriate for all righteous proselytes: "May the Lord recompense your effort; may your reward be complete from the Lord, the God of Israel, under Whose wings you have come to take refuge."[57]

---

[57] Ruth 2:11–12.